WILD LIVES

HORSEBACK CULTURES FROM
IDAHO TO INDONESIA

Contents

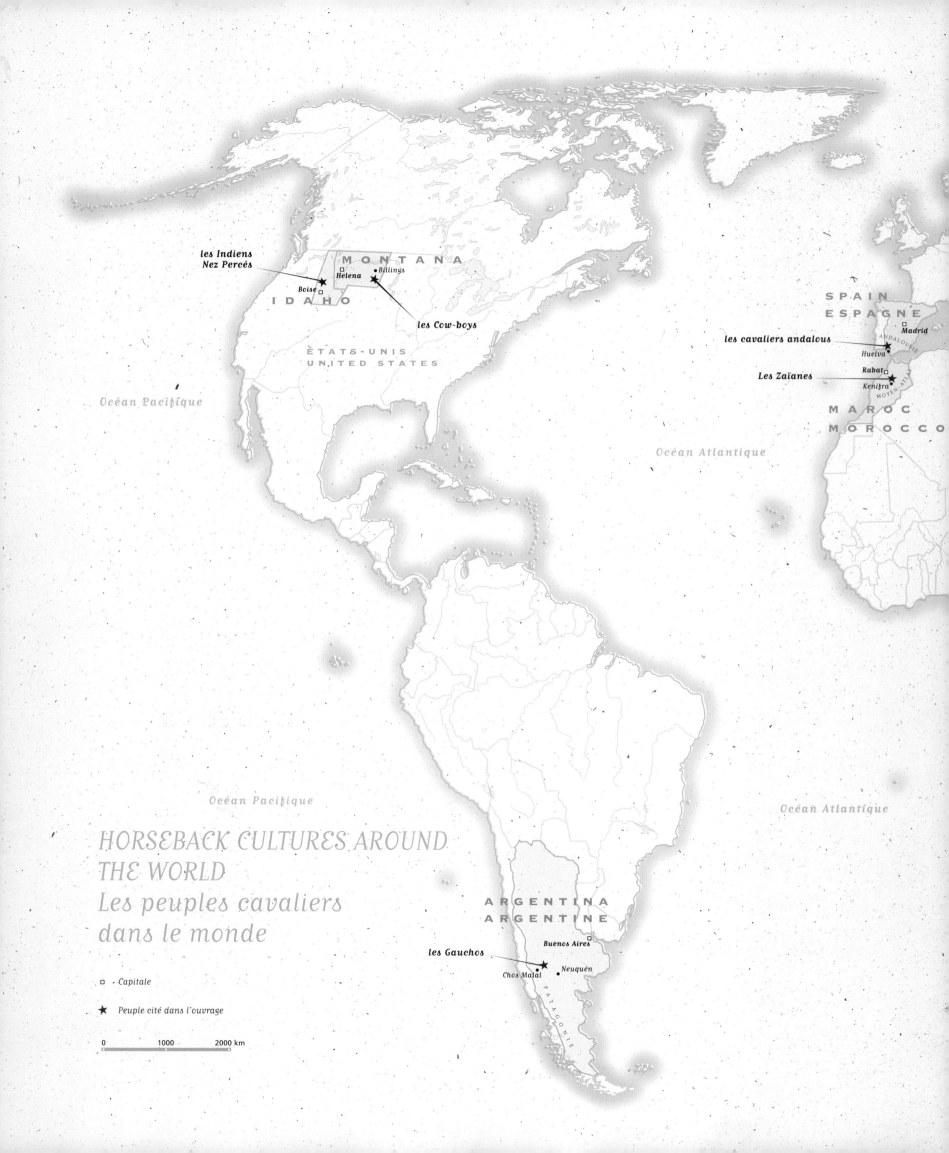

les Indiens
Nez Percés

M O N T A N A

☐ Helena   • Billings

Boise ☐

I D A H O

les Cow-boys

ÉTATS-UNIS
UNITED STATES

Océan Pacifique

S P A I N
E S P A G N E

les cavaliers andalous

ANDALOUSIE

☐ Madrid

Huelva •

Les Zaïanes

Rabat ☐
Kenifra •

MOYEN-ATLAS

M A R O C
M O R O C C O

Océan Atlantique

Océan Pacifique

Océan Atlantique

HORSEBACK CULTURES AROUND
THE WORLD
Les peuples cavaliers
dans le monde

A R G E N T I N A
A R G E N T I N E

les Gauchos

Buenos Aires

Neuquén •

Chos Malal •

P A T A G O N I E

☐ - Capitale

★ - Peuple cité dans l'ouvrage

0   1000   2000 km

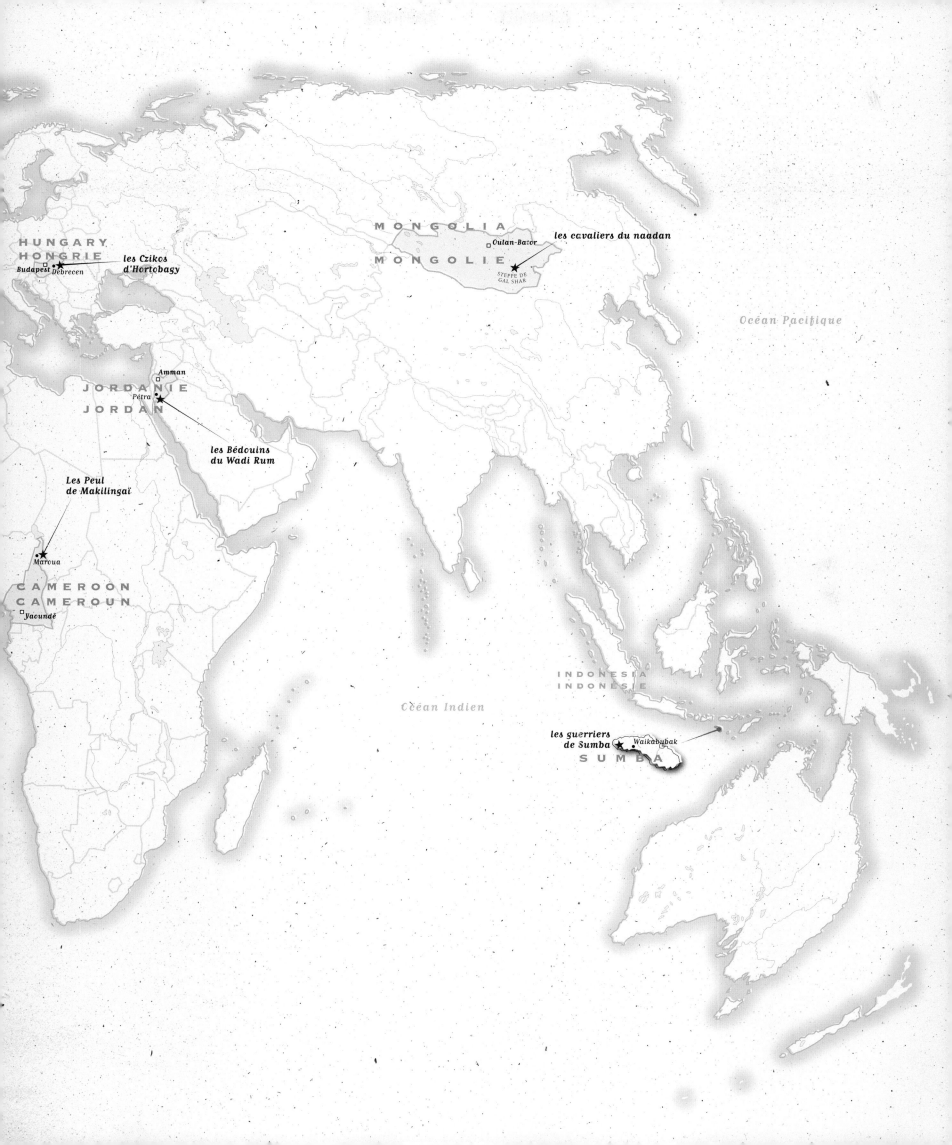

HUNGARY
HONGRIE **les Czikos**
□ Budapest • Debrecen **d'Hortobagy**

MONGOLIA
MONGOLIE
□ Oulan-Bator **les cavaliers du naadan**
STEPPE DE
GAL SHAR

Océan Pacifique

□ Amman
JORDANIE
JORDAN • Pétra
**les Bédouins
du Wadi Rum**

**Les Peul
de Makilingaï**

• Maroua

CAMEROON
CAMEROUN
□ Yaoundé

INDONESIA
INDONÉSIE

Océan Indien

**les guerriers
de Sumba** ★ • Waikabubak
S U M B A

Introduction

Whenever I am on horseback, I think of the first person who introduced me to the world of those who live and breathe horses. He said to me, 'You must meld with the horse, be so much at one with it that you can even feel the ground beneath its hooves. That's the way you'll become a true horseman.' This is the story of the people of the world who experience life through horses.

TIBO

His name was Mumbo. He was an Arabian Barb born near Casablanca in Morocco, just as I was. He had a large head and his coat was a dusty grey. Standing in repose, he always rested one back hoof after the exertion of carrying us on his back — we were youngsters who belonged to the Tit-Melil riding club. I only came up to his shoulder, and I would lay my cheek there to breathe in his strong, peppery smell, a smell that I've seldom encountered since. I remember all my childlike ploys to avoid washing my hands after my ride, and I would think of him even in my dreams. Mumbo was the horse I rode for my first riding lesson, when I was six years old. I would grasp his perpetually tangled mane, sliding my fingers between the strands of hair and locking them round the knots to help me stay on. Although he died a long time ago, Mumbo still carries me on his back in my dreams. He set me on a lifelong path, he was a horse who loved people and he had such a wonderful character.

This book is dedicated to Mumbo.

SYLVIE LEBRETON

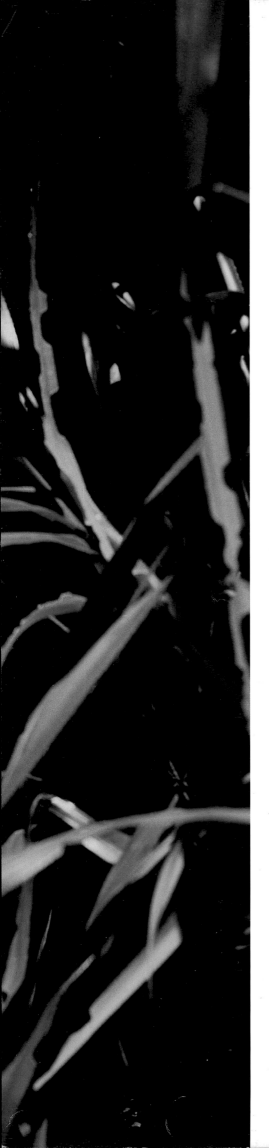

The Warriors of Sumba

BENEATH THE DENSE VEGETATION THAT COVERS THE INDONESIAN ISLAND OF SUMBA THE HEAT IS STIFLING. MATTHIAS AND HIS NEPHEW NELLYS ARE USED TO IT, FOR THEY WERE BORN, 20 YEARS APART, ON THIS ISLAND SITUATED IN THE EASTERN INDIAN OCEAN. RIDJA, THE HORSE THAT MATTHIAS MOST OFTEN RIDES, WAS BORN NOT FAR FROM THE VILLAGE OF TARUNG, ON THE LUSH HILLSIDES WHERE *aling-aling,* A NOURISHING TYPE OF GRASS, GROWS IN ABUNDANCE. RIDJA IS A SMALL HORSE WITH A DAINTY HEAD AND A BROAD FOREHEAD, BOTH OF WHICH SIGNIFY ARAB BLOOD.

ABOVE:

'ON THE ISLAND OF SUMBA, THE MOST IMPORTANT ANIMALS ARE BUFFALO AND HORSES. TO OBTAIN PERMISSION TO MARRY A YOUNG GIRL, THE SUITOR MUST OFFER HER FAMILY A HORSE AS A GIFT. AT THE FUNERAL OF A MAN OF NOBLE BIRTH HIS HORSE IS SACRIFICED SO THAT HE CAN RIDE IN THE AFTERLIFE AND GO WHEREVER HE WISHES IN THE KINGDOM OF HEAVEN. IN OUR VILLAGES THE GRAVES OF ARISTOCRATIC FAMILIES ARE DECORATED WITH HORSES CARVED IN STONE.' MATTHIAS

OPPOSITE PAGE:

A RAINMAKER, A PRIEST WHO COMMUNICATES WITH THE SPIRITS SO AS TO BRING RAIN.

Arab sailors and traders with cargoes of ivory and spices first came to the islands of the Indonesian archipelago in the 6th century, and by the 16th century, Islam had become the region's main religion. There were horses on Sumba even before the Arabs arrived. They were similar to those descended from the prehistoric wild horses of central Asia, but interbreeding with Arab stallions produced a small horse of more slender build. The breed became known as Sandalwood, because Sumba was called Sandalwood Island by early Europeans who visited it to collect the valuable timber of the same name.

Ridja is a Sandalwood. He has great stamina and can cover stony tracks and marshland with equal ease. Matthias owns several horses, but he is particularly fond of Ridja because his father received a good omen about him during a religious rite. The traditional religion of Sumba is a form of animism known as *Marapu*. Animism involves the belief that all natural phenomena are endowed with life or 'spirit'. The Sumbans also believe that the spirits of the ancestors influence the living and can 'govern people and determine the order of things'.

On Sumba, horses have a very important place in social relationships; Wanga, the horse that Nellys usually rides, was a gift to Matthias from his future son-in-law when he came to ask Matthias for his daughter's hand in marriage.

This morning, the two men have been training their horses for the *Pasola*, a ritual battle, that is held once a year. Tomorrow, with all the other horsemen of their village, they will set off to confront another mounted army on the sacred plain of *Tempat Pasola*. But Nellys is worried, yesterday evening it was full moon and his wife Rosvina should have given birth.

Matthias and his nephew are returning to their village which is hidden amidst an outcrop of rocky crags. The men are tired and eager to reach home but the horses are still full of energy, and Ridja dances between roots that stretch across the path and scampers over the stones on the river bed. Their energy comes from grazing the most lush pastures for the last two months, something that Matthias thinks will bring them to peak fitness for the *Pasola*.

Now the house comes into view. It stands on four carved stilts and is crowned by a tall cone of thatch. The two riders dismount and, leading their horses, climb a flight of stone steps. Other houses stand around, creating a central courtyard populated with bas-relief sculptures of horses and people. A young boy hurries up to bring Nellys the news, Rosvina is about to give birth. Matthias leads the horses into the stable and takes off their bridles. The houses contain stables on the ground floor while the family lives on the first floor. The second floor, beneath the roof, is a sacred area where food is stored

'WE USUALLY TRY TO FINISH ALL OUR WORK BEFORE THE *Pasola* STARTS, ESPECIALLY THE WORK IN THE FIELDS, SUCH AS PLOUGHING AND PLANTING RICE. WE GIVE OURSELVES TIME TO PREPARE, THEN, WHEN THE *Pasola* BEGINS, WE CAN FORGET ALL OUR EVERYDAY CARES AND FEEL FULL OF ENERGY.' MATTHIAS

OPPOSITE PAGE:
TURBANS ARE MADE UP OF AROUND EIGHT METRES OF MATERIAL AND YOUNG BOYS ARE GIVEN HELP IN WINDING THEM BY THE OLDER MEN IN THE VILLAGE.

FOLLOWING PAGES:
THE SUMBANS ALWAYS BUILD THEIR HOUSES ON HIGHER LAND SO AS TO PROTECT THE INHABITANTS FROM POSSIBLE ATTACK BY THE PEOPLE OF OTHER VILLAGES.

ON SUMBA, ANYONE CROSSING THE THRESHOLD MUST CORDIALLY SHARE BETEL OR ARECA NUTS. CHEWING THEM IS A SIGN OF HAVING REACHED SEXUAL AND PSYCHOLOGICAL MATURITY. A REFUSAL IS SEEN AS SERIOUSLY OFFENSIVE AND IN THE PAST, THIS VIOLATION OF GOOD MANNERS WAS PUNISHED BY BEHEADING.

and where the precious possessions of the dead are locked away – this is also where the spirit of the *Marapu*, or ancestor, dwells.

Matthias enters his house through a door on the right, this side is reserved exclusively for men, the women's entrance is on the left-hand side of the house. There is a single room with a hearth. Matthias feels like sleeping, but he must prepare his horse's tack for the *Pasola*. Seated cross-legged with the other men of the village, he starts to weave the coconut fibre and feather decorations for his horse's headpiece. Later in the afternoon they will go down to the river. The Sumbans and their horses enjoy swimming in the river. It is in the water that young horses are broken in, the process is gentle and straightforward. When the horse is a year old, it is led into water that is deep but where it can still stand. A young child, the lightest in the village, then climbs onto its back. As it struggles to get out of the water, the horse is unaware of the extra weight on its back. Matthias gets up, adjusting the *parang* (machete) held in the belt of his loincloth, and goes down to the horses to check that their water and hay are fresh.

Matthias puts his horses' comfort above his own or that of his family. Standing peacefully in their stables, the horses are unaware of the importance of the coming *Pasola*. The whole community's prosperity and reputation will rest on their bravery, their speed and their stamina.

Every rider's duty is to uphold the honour of his village. He will be admired for his strategy, for his daring and especially for his skill in throwing his javelin and scoring a hit on his adversary with it. The horses, however, must not be harmed. If a warrior accidentally wounds a horse with his spear, he is banned.

Matthias drinks a little water, precious water that he hopes will be brought in abundance by the next monsoon. Then a cry makes him start, Nellys's son is finally born. His tiny fist was caught up in the umbilical cord, so that he has come into the world with his little shoulder curved backwards, in the attitude of a spear-thrower.

This is a good omen. The spirit of the *Marapu* has given the village a future warrior.

SUMBA IS PROBABLY THE ONLY PLACE IN THE WORLD WHERE THE RIDER MOUNTS HIS HORSE FROM THE RIGHT, THE LEFT BEING CONSIDERED IMPURE.

'WHEN A HORSE IS A YEAR OLD, IT IS LED INTO DEEP WATER WITH A SMALL CHILD ON ITS BACK. THIS IS DONE SEVERAL TIMES, SO THAT THE HORSE BECOMES USED TO CARRYING SOMEONE.' MATTHIAS

FOLLOWING PAGES:
ON SUMBA, IT IS BELIEVED THAT THERE ARE WORDS THAT MAKE THE HEAVENS WEEP. PRIESTS RECITE THESE INCANTATIONS WHILE WALKING, IN THE BELIEF THEY WILL BRING RAIN.

THE *PASOLA*

In the language of Sumba, *pa* means 'lone man' and *sola* 'wooden javelin'. The *Pasola* is a tournament featuring mounted combat between the inhabitants of different villages. In the past, tribal wars would break out on the slightest pretext. A mere disagreement on the size of a wife's dowry was enough to sour relations with a neighbouring village, and quarrels were resolved only by mortal combat. In the 17th century, Jesuit missionaries brought Christianity to South-East Asia and in Indonesia they encouraged the Sumbans to hold an annual joust, the *Pasola*, to resolve that year's conflicts. However, the *Pasola* still sometimes involve fatalities, and as a result, the Indonesian government recently banned the use of steel-tipped spears and wooden javelins.

'*Ikat* IS A TYPE OF COTTON FABRIC COLOURED WITH NATURAL DYES THAT HAS A SOCIAL AND RELIGIOUS MEANING. IT IS WORN AT WEDDINGS AND FOR THE *Pasola*, BUT IT IS ALSO USED AS A SHROUD. THE ONE SHOWN HERE HAS AN ABSTRACT PATTERN BUT MOST *ikats* HAVE TRADITIONAL DESIGNS, WITH COCKERELS, CROCODILES, DRAGONS, SYMBOLS OF WOMANHOOD AND MOST ESPECIALLY HORSES.' ROSVINA

Referees armed with guns monitor the battles, ready to step in if the fighting gets out of control. Astride their superbly decorated horses, the riders wear the traditional *kaïen* or *ikat*, a piece of material tied around the hips. At the waist, they slip through the fearsome *parang*, a machete with an ivory or horn handle that is passed down from father to son. The *Pasola* is an important part of Sumban fertility rites. A few days before the event, the priests go to a sacred beach to collect *nyales* in the sand. These are sea worms that are believed to be strands of the hair of Nyale, beautiful daughter of the moon, who was given to men to assure them plentiful crops and whose body was cut into pieces and thrown into the sea.

THE FIRST WARRIOR OPENS THE COMBAT. IT FOLLOWS A SET PATTERN LIKE A DIVINE DANCE IN WHICH THE DUST RAISES THE SPIRITS OF THE DEAD. SPEARS CLEAVE THE AIR AND THE HORSES' HOOVES DRUM LIKE THUNDER ON THE EARTH.

The greater the harvest of *nyales* on the beach, the more abundant will be the harvest on land. If the *nyales* are scarce, the *Pasola* requires fierce fighting to rouse the gods and human blood must flow to make the ground fertile. A horse's blood, however, must never be spilt or bad fortune will befall the village. The plain where the battles take place is known as the *Tempat Pasola*. In a series of charges, the combatants throw their *tombaks* (spears) with astounding skill. Small clusters of horsemen then launch attacks on their counterparts. They are formidably fierce even though they ride without a saddle, and therefore have no stirrups to help them balance or throw their spears with extra impetus. The fighting extends throughout the day and is enjoyed as a commemoration of the warlike way of the Sumban ancestors.

'THIS *Pasola* WAS MUCH BETTER FOR US THAN THE ONE HELD LAST YEAR. OUR OPPONENTS HAD MORE HORSES THAN WE DID, BUT WE FOUGHT MORE BRAVELY AND FORTUNATELY, ALTHOUGH BLOOD WAS SHED, NO-ONE DIED. THAT AUGURS WELL FOR THE HARVEST.' NELLYS

'IT IS DIFFICULT TO UNDERSTAND HOW PEOPLE CAN BE
SO DIFFERENT, YET SO SIMILAR.'
LA ROCHEFOUCAULD, *Maxims*

The Horsemen of Andalusia

IT IS STILL EARLY SPRING BUT, AS DAWN BREAKS, THE PROMISE OF A HOT DAY IS ALREADY IN THE AIR. AN EERIE STILLNESS LIES ON THE ANDALUSIAN PLAINS. THE EASTERLY BREEZE HAS ALMOST DIED DOWN AND SHADOWS TINGED WITH BLUE BEGIN TO TAKE SHAPE BENEATH THE CORK OAKS. PEDRO HAS JUST DISMOUNTED. SLIGHTLY SQUINTING INTO THE DISTANCE, HE SCOURS THE HORIZON ALL AROUND. FIRST HE LOOKS NORTH, TOWARDS THE SIERRA MORENA THAT RISES BEYOND HUELVA, THE TOWN WHERE HE WAS BORN. HE SEEMS PUZZLED BUT, PURSING HIS LIPS, HE LETS OUT A LONG WHISTLE — A CALL TO HIS MARES. BESIDE HIM STANDS HUELVENO, HIS FAVOURITE STALLION, WHO IS STARING ALERTLY INTO THE DISTANCE.

As they were both born here, the man and his horse have an inborn knowledge of these lands. Pedro waits, knowing that his father and Miguel, the horse breeder, will soon arrive.

Pedro savours moments of solitude, especially here, at this stud devoted to Spanish thoroughbreds. Horses have always been a part of his life, and he loves them intensely and profoundly. As he takes in their rounded, muscular rumps, their short, well-proportioned backs and their silky coats of silvery grey that whiten as the horses age, he is filled with love. In such precious moments of intimacy with horses he can admire their broad, deep chests, stroke their strong necks and savour the musky scent that surrounds them in their boxes. He would willingly spend every night with his hands entangled in their thick manes. Pedro breathes deeply and, turning towards Huelveno, lays his hand on the horse's muzzle, stroking its silky nostrils with his fingers.

Pedro has just turned 16. The Andalusian countryside and the Spanish thoroughbred are his heritage. In their honour he likes to dress in traditional Andalusian costume. Its grey tones – matching the grey horses – sit well with the ochre glow of leather, the colour of the earth. Pedro feels warm breath on his forearm and looks up at Huelveno, with a surge of pride. The stallion is a Spanish thoroughbred, not an Andalusian, as foreigners are in the habit of calling the breed. The name goes back to the days when

PREVIOUS PAGE, RIGHT: LOOKING LIKE MASAI WARRIORS, THE SHADOWS OF THESE HORSEMEN APPEAR TO DRIVE THE CALF THROUGH THE EARLY MORNING SUNLIGHT.

Haute école IS EQUESTRIANISM DEVELOPED INTO A FINE ART. HORSE AND RIDER ACHIEVE A MUTUAL UNDERSTANDING THAT ALLOWS THE HORSE TO MOVE ELEGANTLY AND GRACEFULLY IN RESPONSE TO BARELY PERCEPTIBLE AIDS FROM THE RIDER. 'THE SPANISH THOROUGHBRED IS BY NATURE RESPONSIVE AND INTELLIGENT. HE IS BRIGHT-EYED, HE SEES THINGS IN THE SAME WAY THAT WE DO, AND HE WANTS TO DO WHAT WE ASK OF HIM.' PEDRO

ABOVE RIGHT: PEDRO, AGED 13, PROUDLY WEARING THE TRADITIONAL ANDALUSIAN HORSEMAN'S COSTUME.

'WHEN SCHOOLING FIRST BEGINS, THE RELATIONSHIP BETWEEN A RIDER AND A HORSE IS OFTEN FILLED WITH TENSION. AS TIME GOES ON, HORSE AND RIDER COME TOGETHER. WITHOUT THE DEVELOPMENT OF HARMONY, NEITHER SCHOOLING NOR *haute école* WOULD BE POSSIBLE.' PEDRO JOSÉ CALÉRO FLORES, PEDRO'S FATHER

almost the whole of the Iberian peninsula was under Moorish rule and was known as Andalusia. A smile spreads over the young man's face, to him, as long as the horses from his native Andalusia are known all over the world, it does not matter what name they are given. The Spanish horse is a bewitching creature. Everyone who sees it falls under its spell, captivated by the animal's power and beauty, and impressed by its distinguished past.

The invaders who overran Spain after the fall of the Roman Empire set about making the Spanish horse their most highly prized possession in order to glorify their victories and to affirm their supremacy. Spain was invaded by the Visigoths in the 5th century. These barbarians had strong, heavy horses but far preferred the swift and sure-footed Spanish stallions for their cavalry.

The Carthusian monks of Jerez, Seville and Castille began seriously breeding the Spanish thoroughbred in the 15th century. In 1700, they inaugurated the first stud book, giving the breed the name *Cartujano*, a word that means 'Carthusian' in Spanish.

her haughty bearing confirms her distant origins. Her sire is Panadéro and her dam Jota, both of whom are descended from the famous *Cartujanos*.

Huelveno paws the ground, anxious to gallop, but Pedro hands the reins to Francisco, he wants to go up to the little filly and give her a name. He turns to Miguel and announces that he will call her Reconquista, meaning the Reconquest. Miguel smiles. The meaning is clear, the birth of this filly, at the dawn of the 21st century, in the native birthplace of the Spanish thoroughbred, symbolises the great influence that the horses have made over the centuries. Their finest and most sublime qualities have been passed on to their descendants which have included many different breeds: the Lipizzaner, Aztec, Lusitano, Welsh Cob, Connemara, and American mustang are all descended from the steed of the Spanish Conquistadors – the Andalusian, or more accurately, the Spanish thoroughbred.

Standing on legs almost as long as her mother's, Reconquista proudly surveys the plains of Andalusia. One day, she too may produce a foal and continue her noble bloodline.

PREVIOUS PAGE:
ARMED WITH LONG POLES KNOWN AS *garrochas*,
THE HORSEMEN TEACH THEIR MOUNTS HOW TO
HERD AND SEPARATE STOCK OR WILD HORSES.
THIS IS THE ART OF *doma vaquera*.

ABOVE:
AS THE HORSES THUNDER THROUGH THE STREETS
OF THE VILLAGE OF EL ROCIO, A VOICE RISES ABOVE
THE DIN AND A HERDER SHOUTS, 'CLEAR THE WAY
FOR THE KINGS OF THE PEOPLE.' FRANCISCO AND
GARIADOR, HIS GREY HORSE, KEEP A WATCHFUL
EYE ON THE PASSING CAVALCADE.

'THE HERDERS' VOICES CARRY ON THE WIND IN
THE MARSHES... AND THE HERD OF HORSES WERE
PASSING THROUGH UNTIL DAWN.' FOLKSONG

THE MARES OF EL ROCIO

ABOVE:
THE MEN HAVE A WEEK IN WHICH
TO BUY AND SELL HORSES. 'SOME
FOALS ARE SOLD. THOSE THAT
ARE NOT HAVE THEIR MANES
TRIMMED AND THEY ARE
RETURNED TO THE MARSHLANDS
FOR ANOTHER YEAR.' PEDRO

RIGHT:
IT TAKES FIVE PEOPLE TO
MANOEUVRE OBSERVADOR,
A FOAL THAT IS LITTLE MORE
THAN ONE MONTH OLD.

Near El Rocio, in the province of Huelva, are marshlands known as
Las Marismas. These marshlands, which cover several thousand hectares,
were once owned by breeders of Spanish thoroughbred horses.
The Spanish government ordered that the 'marshland breeders' were
to be expelled from the area so that it could be turned into a nature reserve
which was later called the Doñana National Park. This order did not,
however, expel the breeders' mares, which still roam freely in the park.
The government allows the breeders access to the park for one week each
year. On horseback, the breeders round up the mares and foals, and drive
the great herd to the village of Almonte, where they are assessed, branded
with the mark of their owners and where some are sold. The village has
a state-owned stud, where stallions are kept to cover the mares.

48

'IN ALMONTE, IT IS THE TRADITION TO SELECT
THE BEST MARES FROM THE WILD HERD AND
TO BREED THEM WITH STALLIONS THAT THE
OWNERS PICK FROM A GROUP SPECIALLY
PROVIDED BY THE STATE.' FRANCISCO

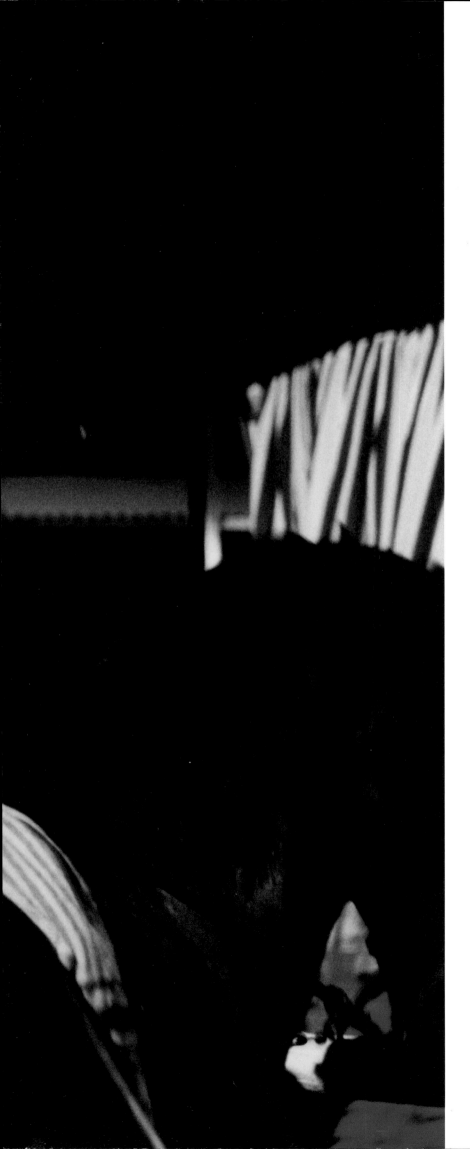

ROMÉRIA AND FÉRIA

In 1960 an epidemic of equine flu swept through all the studs in Spain
and the outbreak was particularly severe in Andalusia. The horse
breeders of Andalusia, usually so ready to take on any challenge, began
to lose hope. Religion, particularly as expressed in religious festivals,
has always been an important part of life in the region and, for the
people of Andalusia, the local fairs, or *ferias*, are a means of celebrating
the mystical relationship between horses, people and religion. The best
way, therefore, of reviving a belief in hope for the future was to ensure
that every village held its annual festival as usual. The festivals are normally
held every weekend throughout the spring and summer and those of small
villages can be equally as splendid as those in the cities of Seville or
Jerez de la Frontera. The festivals include parades, competitions and
demonstrations of riding. *Casetas* – small houses made of wood and
canvas decorated with paper lanterns, embroidered shawls and flowers
– are built specially for the occasion. Families and friends meet to dance,
play the guitar and toast each other with glasses of manzanilla until dawn.
The women, elegant in their flounced dresses, take rides in carriages drawn
by two or three horses, or ride behind their men. The festival ends with
the traditional Spanish treat of a cup of frothy hot chocolate and doughnuts.
Fortunately, severe flu epidemics are now a thing of the past and the
people of Andalusia continue to breed and enjoy their agile, elegant and
courageous horses.

'I CAN'T IMAGINE WHAT ANDALUSIA WOULD BE LIKE
WITHOUT HORSES. IT WOULD BE NOTHING MORE
THAN A GREAT OPEN SPACE WITHOUT LIFE OR
VIBRANCY. HORSES ARE OUR LIFE, OUR WHOLE LIFE.'
PEDRO JOSÉ CALÉRO FLORES

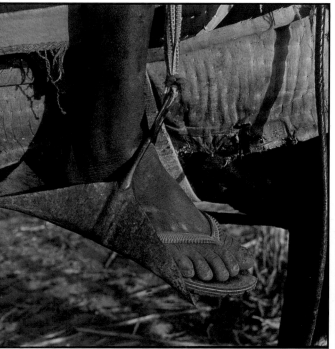

Amadou is a living repository of his tribe's knowledge. He has devoted his life to cattle and horses, and he is the worthy descendant of those ancient nomadic herders who have outlived the rise and fall of numerous African empires.

As he lies on his straw mattress, the old man floats between sleep and the final descent into oblivion, his breathing becoming increasingly shallow. Beneath their furrowed, shrivelled lids, his eyes are closed to the world but he is inwardly looking back over his life. He is wondering whether he was successful in transmitting to his son and his grandson, the story of his ancestors, of which he, as the marabout and wise man, was one of the guardians.

Until the 18th century, the Peul were the poorest and most rootless people of Africa, but horses were to alter the course of their destiny. Their first encounter with these swift and powerful creatures occurred when the Peul were travelling through the Hausa empire, which covered what is now Niger and Nigeria. Already skilled stock breeders and cattle herders, the Peul appropriated the Hausas' horses and soon became invincible warriors. In 1804, a Peul warrrior named Ousmane dan Fodio proclaimed himself 'commander of the faithful' and made himself their war leader. He appointed twelve horsemen and gave them standards. These standard-bearers then set out on a crusade. They conquered Niger, Nigeria, Chad and northern Cameroon, converting their

inhabitants to Islam. Once they had gained control of these countries, the Peul adopted a settled way of life and now live in harmony with the region's other ethnic groups. Any desire to pursue their crusade further north was, in any case, limited by the African terrain – horses are unsuited to equatorial forests and are weakened and even killed by the relentless onslaught of tsetse flies. Without their steeds, the Peul could go no further north.

Once they had settled, the Peul's conquered territories were divided into chiefdoms, each governed by a *lamido*, a headman who was, with the marabout, the guardian of the Peul's culture, traditions and religion. The *lamido* is, traditionally, the only person permitted to own horses outright. He gives them as gifts to noblemen in his entourage who then keep them within their families.

In the elderly Amadou's village, this tradition is upheld. For several generations now, every horse has had its own hut. The women, by contrast, must share a hut with several others of their sex. It is also the women's job to feed and water the horses. Three times a day they go to the well to draw water, a precious commodity for African families. The horses are given unlimited quantities of peanut cuttings and three measures of millet a day. Every care is lavished on the horses, which are held in high esteem by generation after generation of these former nomads and ancient horsemen.

'HORSES HAVE ALWAYS BEEN A PART OF OUR FAMILY, BUT THE ELDERS ARE THE ONLY ONES WHO REALLY KNOW HOW TO LOOK AFTER THEM BECAUSE THEY KNOW HOW TO LISTEN TO THE LANGUAGE THAT HORSES SPEAK. YOUNG PEOPLE NOW ARE ONLY INTERESTED IN MOTORBIKES AND BICYCLES. I'VE TOLD MY SON AND MY GRANDSON THAT HORSES ARE A PART OF OUR CULTURE AND OUR LIFE. THEY ARE AS IMPORTANT AS THE KORAN. IF THEY DON'T UNDERSTAND THAT, THEN MY LIFE HAS BEEN WASTED.' AMADOU, MARABOUT OF MAKILINGAI

LEFT: BAKARI, THE SON OF AMADOU WITH M'BOULOU, HIS LITTLE MARE.

ABOVE: AMADOU PASSES ON HIS KNOWLEDGE TO ABDOU, HIS GRANDSON.

FOLLOWING PAGES: EARLY MORNING IN THE VILLAGE OF MAKILINGAI.

Amadou is stirred from his thoughts by the sound of movement and a sharp crack coming from the neighbouring hut. His face is impassive but his heart warms as he pictures his family's little mare setting off for the bush. A thick sprig from a groundnut probably snapped under her hoof. The old man senses a shadow and smells a scent – she is at the door.

As she does every morning, the mare pokes her head into the old man's hut and looks at this strangely quiet, prostrate shape. As usual, she searches for a few extra grains of millet but this morning something else draws her into the hut. She stretches her neck into the entrance and breathes on the long fingers of his hand, a hand that has never hurt her. As Amadou stays perfectly still, she gets bolder and nuzzles his shoulder, then his neck and gently touches the dying man's forehead with her silky muzzle. Then she backs away and is gone.

Amadou wanted to stroke her. This young filly is the last of that bloodline of horses to have accompanied him through his life and to have shared his own personal history.

Like all Peul, and despite the increasing encroachment of the Western world, Amadou has preserved his people's culture and kept alive the deep reverence that they have always felt for horses.

This regard for horses has been handed down to Abdou, his grandson. Within a short time, the 11-year-old boy has shown extraordinary skill as a horseman. His prowess has been acknowledged by the *lamido* with an official ceremony in which Abdou has been presented with the chiefdom's sacred sword.

Although Amadou, and the entire Peul people, still have a relationship of mutual respect with the horse, this is not always the case with the region's other ethnic groups. The horse, which, until the last century, was considered to be a sign of wealth,

is now all too often treated as a servant. A horse given to a family by the *lamido* may be abandoned in a corner, tied up and hobbled, or even relegated to the role of packhorse.

With long experience of treating sick, mangy or undernourished horses, Amadou is one of the last marabouts who knows how to heal them in traditional ways. He will sometimes bleed a horse by piercing the vein beneath its upper lip. The horses are often asked to do strenuous work, such as galloping over long distances delivering messages to other chiefdoms or pursuing cattle thieves. They also take part in the village fantasias that are organised by the *lamidos*.

The last fantasia that the old man attended was held in Makilingai, his own village. The *lamido* was keen to ensure that the village would be suitably impressive for the occasion; there were flowers everywhere, and all rubbish was cleared from the streets.

MEN HOBBLE HORSES IN ORDER TO FORGET THAT THEY THEMSELVES ARE IN SHACKLES.

The old man remembers seeing groups of riders with spears arriving from the bush to take part in the fantasia. Welcomed by musicians and griots (travelling poets and musicians), and cheered by a crowd in festive mood, their horses paw the ground, dance and rear. Blood-streaked foam runs from their mouths.

The old Arab bits in their mouths have a pointed bar that digs into the horses' palate when it is raised. The riders shout out the *lamido's* name, but His Majesty, Tikire Boukar, is nowhere to be seen; he is out of the public gaze, in the cob-walled confines of his palace. It is midday and the sun beats down. The men dismount. Amadou stands guard beside the large chests brought by servants, they contain the ceremonial attire with which the horses will be adorned for the parade. This will be a celebration of the military history of the tribe's warlike ancestors. In groups of five or six, the horsemen career through the village streets at a gallop, the horses' hooves kicking up a cloud of

THESE MEN SERVE A KING AND ARE ALSO SLAVES TO THEIR HORSES. HOWEVER, THEY ARE DEVOTED TO THEIR CHARGES AND THIS MAKES LIGHT OF THE HARD WORK THEY MUST UNDERTAKE.

UNDER A HOT SUN, A WARRIOR AND HIS HORSE
PATIENTLY AWAIT THE *lamido's* COMMAND.

yellow dust. The warriors brandish their lances and wooden spears above the heads of
their frantic mounts.

Amadou feels a gentle touch on his shoulder. He returns to the present, but it is for the
last time. His son is beside him, speaking to him in a trembling voice. The little mare is
behaving oddly, and the women are worried. Old Amadou feels a gentle warmth sweep
over him. His son has just told him that the mare did not go out into the bush as usual;
she is still here, just outside the old marabout's hut. The lore of the ancestors insists that
man cannot travel on the earth or in the afterlife without a horse. Amadou understands,
he moves his right hand feebly. He wants to tell his son that the mare's unusual
behaviour is a sign for him that his time has come, but he does not have the strength to
speak. His journey to the afterlife must begin. Amadou suddenly experiences a strange
sensation. His legs feel the familiar soft, warm animal silkiness and he seems to be
astride that mass of moving muscles. As he sets off on his last ride, lovingly and trust-
ingly, he lets himself be carried. Outside the hut, the little mare starts to walk away.

THE FANTASIA

On grand festive occasions, the people of Cameroon hold fantasias in memory of the ancient horsemen of Islam. Festivals are also held to welcome a dignitary, enthrone a chief or mark the end of Ramadan. Horses once again take pride of place in the affairs of the people. They are covered in strings of colourful pompoms and glistening armour. During the opening parade, the *lamido*, in sacred attire and escorted by his cavalry, makes his appearance on a horse. The heavy armour is then taken off the other horses so that they can gallop. Then, as the villagers dance to the rhythm of the drums and the singing of the griots, the cavalry charge begins with successive waves of riders, carrying spears or swords, galloping up to the throne where the *lamido* is seated.

'ISLAM IS A GREAT CAVALCADE'. ACCORDING TO THE KORAN, THE HORSE HAS A SACRED ROLE. BY TREATING THEIR STEEDS WITH RESPECT, MEN THEREFORE HONOUR GOD.

FOLLOWING PAGES: THE FURIOUS CHARGE OF A FANTASIA EVOKES THE FIERCE BATTLES OF AN ISLAMIC ARMY, WHO FOR THEIR CONQUESTS RELIED AS MUCH ON THEIR HORSES AS ON THEIR SWORDS.

According to Peul legend, the red colour
of the sky at dusk is caused by sparks flying
from the hooves of horses as they gallop
away with the souls of their dead masters.
The sparks light the way through the
darkness of the underworld and lead the
horses towards the divine light.

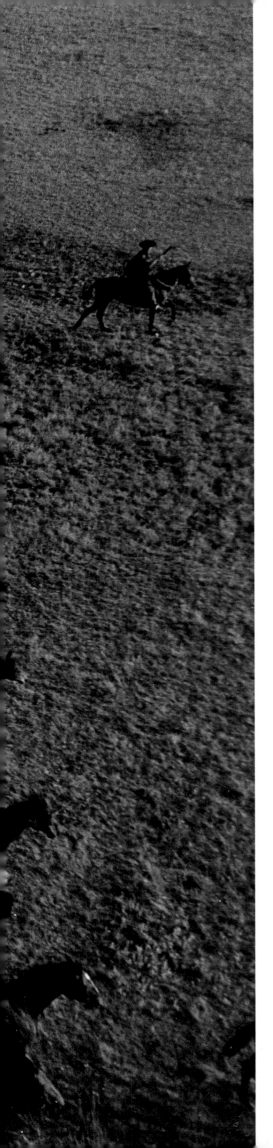

The Czikos of Hortobagy

ITSVAN IS GETTING MARRIED! AS DANIEL PUTS THE TELEPHONE DOWN, THE IMPORTANCE OF THIS PIECE OF NEWS SLOWLY SINKS IN. TOMORROW, HIS BEST FRIEND ITSVAN IS COMING TO INTRODUCE HIM TO HIS FIANCÉE. THIS IS ASTONISHING NEWS, BUT DANIEL CANNOT REPRESS A SMILE. LIKE ITSVAN, HE IS 20 YEARS OLD, BUT IF HE EVER MARRIES IT WOULD HAVE TO BE TO A WOMAN PREPARED TO DEVOTE HER LIFE TO THE NONIUS, THE FAMOUS BAY HORSES OF THE HUNGARIAN *Puszta*.

Born 120 miles (200 km) east of Budapest, Daniel and Itsvan grew up on the Hortobagy *Puszta*, the Hungarian steppe. They learnt to ride horses near the Carpathian Mountains, they both dreamt of becoming great Czikos, literally, 'breeders of foals' and they solemnly vowed to devote their whole lives to horses.

Lajos, Daniel's uncle, is a renowned horse trainer and also a superb rider. As he sits watching a horse being schooled, his thoughts turn to the next generation, to whom he would like to entrust the wisdom of the Czikos. He is glad that Daniel shares his passion for horses, and he is currently teaching him the Hungarian way of training them. Lajos rises to his feet and goes over to Magyar, a young horse of just six years old. In Hungary, horses are not trained until they have reached physical maturity and Magyar is just approaching this age. One important lesson for the young horse is to lie down on the rider's command. To teach him, Lajos has slipped a long rope around his off-side (right) front hoof and, resting a hand on the horse's side, he pats him, speaks to him and walks around him. Then, gently pressing the horse's left shoulder, he twitches the top of its near-side (left) hind hoof with the end of his spurred boot, gently pulling the rope with his right hand at the same time.

Magyar is a genuine Hungarian Nonius. Tractable and willing to please, he has a calm expression but is always alert.

PREVIOUS PAGES: ALMOST ALL NONIUS HORSES ARE BAY, BUT BECAUSE THE BREED CARRIES ARAB BLOOD, AN OCCASIONAL GREY FOAL IS BORN.

ABOVE: USING A LENGTH OF ROPE, THE TRAINER GENTLY RAISES ONE OF THE HORSE'S LEGS AND THEN PUSHES AT THE SHOULDER TO ENCOURAGE IT TO LEARN TO LIE DOWN ON COMMAND.

THE CZIKOS' PHILOSOPHY IS BASED ON A RELATIONSHIP OF TRUST WITH THE HORSE. 'THE HORSE MUST BECOME PARTNERS WITH ITS RIDER, JUST LIKE A HUSBAND IS PARTNER TO HIS WIFE.' LAJOS

FOLLOWING PAGES:
TRAINING IS GENTLE AND CONSIDERATE TO THE HORSE. THE HORSE LEARNS TO RESPOND TO THE RIDER'S VOICE AND IS NEVER SUBJECTED TO THE USE OF WHIP OR SPURS.

Daniel's favourite tale is the story of the breed. From the age of five, when they used to go fishing together, he would demand that his uncle tell him once more the incredible story of a stallion called Nonius Senior. Lajos would always begin the story the same way, 'Nonius Senior was born in France. At the time, Napoleon was the Emperor of France, and Hungary was in the Austrian Empire. One day, when Napoleon was on his campaign in Russia, our cavalry invaded France. A Hungarian general who adored horses went to the stud in Rosières and saw Nonius Senior in the yard. He was a dark bay Anglo-Norman with a dark brown mane and tail. Nonius Senior was just two years old, and the French, who preferred Spanish horses, didn't like him. They thought his eyes were too small, his head too large and his back too long. But the general decided to take Nonius Senior back with him to Hungary because the stallion was so gentle. For over 20 years he lived in Debrecen, in the Mezöhegyes stud, where he died in 1832. Nonius Senior was an incredible horse – whatever the breed of the mares that were put to him, all the foals that he sired were the image of him. Not only that, but his foals also went on to produce identical offspring. The stud managers soon saw that Nonius Senior was a remarkable horse and had generated a new breed. There is a legend that if a horseman is out on the steppe and hears a horse's whinny before sunrise, it is the great Nonius Senior himself, and his whinny means that, so long as the Czikos hold horses in esteem, he'll give Hungary as many in his own image as the land can feed.'

All Nonius horses are surprisingly similar in conformation and colour. Later in the 19th century, the Hungarians crossed Nonius horses with English thoroughbreds and Arabs to refine the breed, but almost all the resulting offspring were still bay.

Now, Lajos gently asks the horse to bend its knee, the first stage in teaching it to lie down. Daniel has finally come back and is standing behind him. Silently watching, he is always filled with wonder at the patience and gentleness that Lajos shows. It will soon

be dusk and the two men must bring in the stud's 300 horses, which wander freely over the steppe during the day. In summer, the heat is so fierce that the horses do not eat properly. Twice a day, at dawn and dusk, the Czikos feed them and take them to drink at a well that has been dug on the steppe.

That evening, in a *csarda* (inn) on the steppe, the two men sit eating goulash around a fire. Daniel can't conceal his anxiety. Itsvan will be here tomorrow, and he feels unsure how he will react to the woman who is about to take his friend and brother away from him.

The next morning, the whinnying of the horses in the stables is echoed by the calling of cockerels heralding the dawn. Daniel walks over to the stables to start the daily round. On the way he meets his bareback riding teacher, Atilla, who is harnessing his five mares.

Daniel recently started learning bareback riding. This involves handling five horses at full gallop, from a standing position on their backs. To do this a young man must have

'OUR RIDING OUTFITS ARE VERY LOOSE SO THAT AIR CAN CIRCULATE AND WE CAN STAY COOL IN THE HIGH TEMPERATURES OF SUMMER.' LAJOS

ABOVE:
'OUR SHOES ARE DESIGNED TO HELP US TO STAND ON THE HORSE'S RUMP AT A GALLOP. THE SOLE IS MADE OF SLIGHTLY DAMP SPONGE SO THAT WE DON'T HURT THE HORSE AND ALSO BECAUSE IT GIVES A BETTER GRIP.' ATTILA

reached adulthood and be exceptionally strong and fit. He must be able to master the exacting technique.

The Czikos' prowess in breaking and training horses and in bareback riding is only a part of their work, but it attracts many tourists in summer. The demonstrations they give are an important source of revenue, especially as, since the collapse of communism, Hungarian studs no longer receive a state subsidy, and the horses and the men who work with them face an uncertain future. Daniel is aware of this, but is loath to give up his life with horses. He feels resentment towards Itsvan, who by deciding to get married appears to have betrayed their boyhood vow never to give up working with horses. The sound of a car horn stirs him from his reverie.

Itsvan is here, with a young woman. 'This is Marianne,' he says. 'She's a vet. She looks after the Nonius on the Bugac *Puszta* and I'll be working with her.' Daniel looks disconcerted. 'You didn't think I could survive without horses, did you?' Itsvan adds, teasingly.

HUNGARIAN BAREBACK RIDING

PREVIOUS PAGE:
THE BLACK AND WHITE UNIFORM OF
THE CZIKOS OF THE BUGAC *puszta,*
IN WESTERN HUNGARY.

ABOVE:
THERE IS A LEGEND THAT AN
AUSTRIAN ARTIST PAINTED A
RIDER STANDING UP ON FIVE
GALLOPING HORSES AND THE
HUNGARIAN RIDER, LENAR BELA,
IS REPUTED TO HAVE BEEN
THE FIRST TO SUCCESSFULLY
CARRY OUT THIS FEAT.

Hungarian bareback riding is an acrobatic act in which the rider controls five, or sometimes ten, galloping horses from a standing position on their backs. Some Hungarian horsemen maintain that this skill dates back to Roman times when it was an equestrian feat performed at the imperial games. Another equally plausible explanation dates from more recent history, central Europe has been the site of many wars and Hungary has often found itself at the centre of these power struggles. As a result, the Hungarian army has needed to maintain military outposts and to keep these stocked with munitions and fresh horses – the latter being brought to the outposts in bunches controlled by just one bareback rider.

HORTOBÁGY

PAGES 93 AND 94:
'IN HUNGARIAN BAREBACK RIDING, THE
HORSE AT THE CENTRE OF THE FRONT
THREE LEADS THE WHOLE TEAM. THE
TWO HORSES ON EITHER SIDE OF IT
MUST KEEP PACE, EXACTLY FOLLOWING
ITS STRIDE.' ATTILA

ABOVE AND OPPOSITE PAGE:
TWO CZIKOS DRIVE A HERD OF NONIUS
HORSES TO THE WELL. THE 350-STRONG
HERD LIVES OUT ON THE WILD PLAINS
AROUND THE EPONA STUD, WHICH IS
THE MAIN BREEDING CENTRE IN HUNGARY
FOR THE NONIUS.

THE NONIUS WAS DECLARED THE 'IDEAL HORSE'
AT THE *Universal Exhibition* HELD IN PARIS IN 1900.
IN 1999 UNESCO MADE IT A WORLD HERITAGE
BREED, AND IT IS NOW PROTECTED.

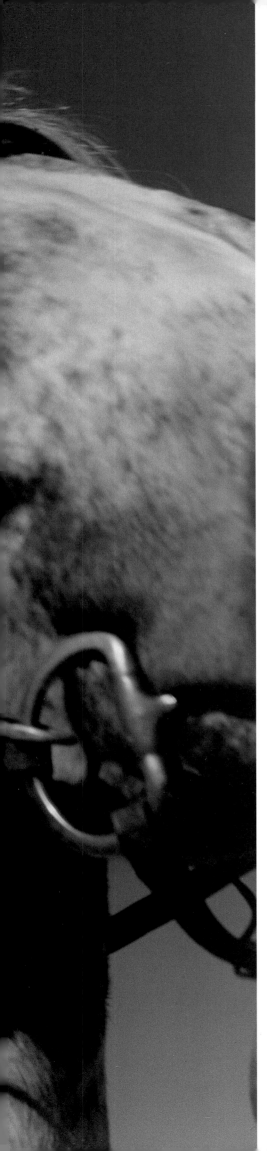

The Nez Percés

CARLA STIRS RESTLESSLY IN HER SLEEP. A DREADFUL CLAMOUR SHATTERS
THE SILENCE OF THE NIGHT. TERRIFIED, CARLA SITS UP; COMING OUT OF THE
WEST, AN AMERICAN CAVALRY UNIT IS SWEEPING OVER THE NATIVE AMERICANS'
LAND. IN A CLOUD OF DUST, THE RIDERS LAY WASTE TO EVERYTHING IN THEIR
PATH, KILLING MEN, WOMEN AND CHILDREN. BLINDED BY TEARS, CARLA MAKES
FOR THE UNCERTAIN SAFETY OF THE FOREST. AS THE SOUND OF GUNSHOTS REND
THE AIR, SHE RUNS. SUDDENLY A GREAT THUNDERING IS HEARD, IT DROWNS OUT
THE GUNSHOTS AND THE CRIES OF THE WOUNDED.

In the fog of smoke and dust, the young woman makes out an enormous shape moving towards her at great speed. She instinctively throws herself to the ground, taking shelter behind a rock. Hundreds of panicking horses, the herd of the Nez Percés, gallop by within an inch of her as they flee the white horsemen, who are deliberately driving them to the edge of a ravine.

Powerless, defeated and brought to her knees, Carla is well aware that without horses her tribe will be unable to put up a fight against the invaders. This, the systematic destruction of the Native Americans' horses, is the toll exacted by the American cavalry as it advances. In the distance, Carla sees the village in flames. She must get to her feet and get back to the survivors but something stops her. Carla hears a whinny. Someone is calling her and a hand shakes her by the shoulder. She tries to sit up with a jerk but the car's seat belt is pinning her down.

Rudy is leaning over her, aware that she is having a nightmare. Rudy and Carla have just arrived at the sacred meeting place. He nods towards the tipis that have already been set up. The Empty Saddles ceremony is due to take place tomorrow. While the Sioux are renowned for hand-to-hand combat, the Comanche for their strategy and the Cheyenne for their bloodthirstiness, the history of the Nez Percés is closely linked to a breed of horse: the Appaloosa.

'WHEN I AM WITH HORSES, I HAVE A SENSE OF WELL-BEING. ALL FEELINGS OF FRUSTRATION LEAVE ME AND I AM IN CLOSER TOUCH WITH MY EMOTIONAL SIDE. I AM PROUD TO BE A NEZ PERCÉ. THE TRADITIONS OF MY TRIBE ARE ANCIENT AND KNOWLEDGEABLE.' CARL RAY PAWAUKEE.

ABOVE:
THE TRADITIONAL NEZ PERCÉ DWELLING WAS A LONG HOUSE COVERED WITH MATS OR SKINS. THE TIPI WAS CONSTRUCTED OF TWELVE WOODEN POLES COVERED BY MATS AND WAS INTENDED TO BE ERECTED AND DISMANTLED SWIFTLY. PERMANENT SETTLEMENTS ALWAYS CONTAINED A SWEAT HOUSE, THE USE OF WHICH WAS CONFINED TO NEZ PERCÉ MEN DURING TRIBAL RITUALS.

government and were confined to a reservation in north-western Idaho. Some Nez Percés, under Chief Joseph, rebelled and refused to relocate to the reservation and were pursued over 1,300 miles (2,000 km) by the US cavalry. Eventually captured and forced to surrender, their horses were destroyed – a policy pursued by the United States government in relation to other tribes. In Kansas, 900 horses belonging to the Cheyenne were massacred near the Washita river, and in 1874, the same fate befell 1,400 horses belonging to the Kiowa and Comanche tribes. The United States government allowed the Nez Percés to keep a few heavy horses for working in the fields but certainly not the magnificent, spotted war horses. There was no chance to resurrect the breed. If a foal was born with anything like an Appaloosa's elegant conformation, it was immediately put to death. This extermination destroyed the soul of a people who had

PREVIOUS PAGE:

SOME WOULD SAY THAT A SOCIETY LIVES ONLY
IF IT CAN GIVE FREE EXPRESSION TO THE
CONTRADICTIONS WITHIN IT. TODAY, THE NEZ
PERCÉS EXIST WITHIN A SPECTRUM THAT
CONTAINS AMERICAN FOOTBALL AND BASEBALL,
AND ALSO TIPIS AND SWEAT HOUSES. THIS
KEEPS THEIR TRADITIONAL CULTURE ALIVE
WHILE ALLOWING THEM FULL ACCESS TO
MODERN AMERICAN LIFE.

NATIVE AMERICANS HAVE A DEEP REVERENCE
FOR THEIR ANCESTORS AND TODAY'S NEZ
PERCÉS BEAR A STRIKING RESEMBLANCE TO
THEIR FOREBEARS. THE CONTINUING VITALITY
OF A CULTURE DEPENDS ON A COMMUNAL
DESIRE TO KEEP ITS ROOTS ALIVE.

lived with Appaloosas for more than 150 years, and recent generations have grown up with little experience of these horses. Then in 1991, some 120 years after the massacre of their horses, a breeder of Appaloosas in New Mexico offered the Nez Percés in the Lapwai reservation 13 of his finest mares.

Carla, a member of the Appaloosa Society, gets out of the car and walks up to a three-year-old stallion, who is saddled and covered with decorations and embroidered rugs. Although she knows the stallion well, she still looks admiringly at him: he is just over 15 hands, his back is strong and compact and his neck is thick. The skin around his nostrils is flecked, the whites of his eyes gleam, and his hooves are striped. Carla talks to the two men, Rudy and Mario – both Nez Percés and members of the Chief Joseph Foundation. Now it is time for everyone to get ready for the ceremony.

Although the Nez Percés are now very Americanised, their daily lives still have a markedly spiritual dimension. The tribe lives in housing in a so-called residential

district, but outside every house there is a tipi and a sweat lodge; this is an important spiritual place where members of the community gather.

As the Empty Saddles ceremony is about to start, Carla's daughter approaches her. Like the men, the two Nez Percé women are here to honour the ancestors killed in the final battle. But, on this symbolic day, Carla has also come to show the members of her tribe the results of her work. She and Rudy are working to create a new breed of horse: the Nez Percé, a cross between an Appaloosa and an Akhal-Teke.

Together, mother and daughter go into their designated tipi. Carla picks up a presentation bridle but, at the entrance, she hands it to her daughter without a word. The tribe's two newest generations will walk hand in hand.

RUDY WATCHES HIS SON WORKING WITH A HORSE. THEY HAVE BOTH INHERITED THE SKILL OF THE 'HORSE WHISPERER' — THIS MEANS BEING ABLE TO COMMUNICATE WITH THE HORSE IN ITS OWN TERMS. 'OUR FOREBEARS LEARNT TO COPY THE BEHAVIOUR OF THE DOMINANT MARE IN THE HERD. YOUR WHOLE RELATIONSHIP WITH THE HORSE DEPENDS ON HOW YOU MAKE EYE CONTACT WITH IT AND HOW AND WHERE YOU STAND IN RELATION TO IT. IF YOU WALK STRAIGHT TOWARDS A HORSE, HE'LL MOVE BACK. IF YOU WALK ROUND IN A CIRCLE TO GET NEAR HIM, HE'LL GET CURIOUS. WE USE THE BODY LANGUAGE OF THE HORSE IN ORDER TO TRAIN IT.' RUDY

PREVIOUS PAGES:
'THERE MAY BE PLACES WHERE SUDDENLY
IT FEELS AS IF YOU'RE IN THE SKY.'
ANDRÉ DHÔTEL, *Mémoires de Sébastien*

ALONGSIDE THE TRAPPINGS OF A
WESTERN LIFESTYLE — PICKUP TRUCKS,
JACKETS AND RAYBANS — TRADITIONAL
COSTUME LIKE THIS BUFFALO-HORN
HEADDRESS STILL HAS ITS PLACE.

EMPTY SADDLES

For the 3,000 surviving Nez Percés, the year is punctuated by acts of commemoration. Victories as well as defeats are marked. The warriors killed on 5 October 1877 are honoured at the Empty Saddles ceremony, held on the first weekend of October. The ritual opens with the whole tribe singing traditional songs, then the peace pipe is passed round. Horses tethered around the tipis are decked out in colourful beadwork and eagle feathers, reflecting the importance that the Native Americans accord them. They are led three times around four dignitaries who wear their finest headdresses. Blankets are laid over the horses' saddles, original Native American saddles made of a wooden frame over which leather is stretched, and these are presented to deserving members of the tribe at the end of the ceremony.

HEADDRESSES ARE BROUGHT TO BE LAID AT THE FEET OF FOUR DIGNITARIES AT THE EMPTY SADDLES CEREMONY.

117

AS THE HORSE DESCRIBES THREE SACRED
CIRCLES AROUND THE DIGNITARIES, THE LITTLE
GIRL LISTENS TO A SPEECH GIVEN BY HER
MOTHER, CARLA. 'IN MEMORY AND IN HONOUR
OF OUR PEOPLE. SO THAT OUR CHILDREN MAY
ALSO CARRY AND PASS ON THIS PRIDE, THIS LOVE,
AND THIS MEMORY. SO THAT WHEN WE RETURN
TO THIS PLACE 120 YEARS FROM NOW, HORSES WILL
STILL BE PART OF OUR HERITAGE.' CARLA HIGH EAGLE

The Cowboys of Montana

FROM BEYOND THE MOUNTAINS, THE SOUND OF STEEL BLADES CARRIED ON THE WIND REACHES TRAVIS'S EARS, BUT HE HARDLY LOOKS UP. AS FOUR HELICOPTERS MOVE ACROSS THE SKY, THE YOUNG MAN IS SEIZED BY THE DESIRE TO PRESS HIS CHEEK AGAINST HIS HORSE'S WARM, REASSURING NECK. AUTUMN HAS ARRIVED, AND THE FRAGRANT PLAINS OF MONTANA HAVE TURNED TO GOLD. SHEPHERDED BY DOGS AND DRIVEN BY RIDERS, THE FIRST HERDS REACH THE CORRALS. THERE ARE STILL 800 ANIMALS UP THERE IN THE MOUNTAINS, WHERE THEY ROAM FREE FOR MUCH OF THE YEAR. NOW, IN THE GREAT AUTUMN ROUND-UP, THEY WILL BE BROUGHT DOWN.

PREVIOUS PAGES:
'WE USUALLY ASK OUR NEIGHBOURS
TO COME OVER AND HELP US WITH THE
AUTUMN ROUND-UP. IT'S A TIME OF
CELEBRATION IN THE YEAR AND A GOOD
WAY OF PREPARING FOR THE HARD
WINTER WORK AHEAD.' EARL

THE HORSES WEAR STUDDED SHOES,
WHICH GIVES THEM A FIRMER GRIP IN
THE SNOW. THIS IS A CHANCE FOR EARL
TO SHOW TRAVIS THE FINER POINTS OF
WINTER SHOEING.

With his two dogs, Travis hurries to join Earl, his grandfather, who owns the ranch. The reassuring clinking of bits signals that the horses in their boxes are saddled and ready to go. As he shoes a horse, Earl jokes about all those herders who have fallen into the trap of mechanisation. Neither he nor his family want to give up their horses, even though many American ranchers now use motor vehicles to round the animals up.

It is seven o'clock in the morning, and other riders arrive at the ranch, warmly dressed against the cold. Every autumn, these friends come with their dogs and horses to help with the round-up. At this ranch, the round-up happens at a leisurely pace and, thanks to the Quarter Horse, the work is done in the time-honoured way. A cross between the Spanish purebred and the English thoroughbred, the Quarter Horse was the first wholly American breed. Renowned for its speed over short distances, it was bred especially to race over a quarter of a mile, hence its name. The only horses in the world capable of reaching a speed of 30 miles (50 km) over a this distance, they are also used in longer

law in those days meant that any cattle that had not been branded were public property. Travis would have so loved to round up all the livestock he could find, and to gallop after cattle and the wild horses in the mountains! Large herds of cattle and horses had roamed free here ever since the 16th century, when European settlers, wandering across the unknown lands of the New World, had accidentally allowed thousands of cattle and horses to escape.

Today, there are far fewer wild horses. Ranches are gradually disappearing, replaced by farms rearing cattle by intensive methods. Travis knows how lucky he is. Though he is living in the third millennium, he is still a cowboy on a working ranch.

After riding for two hours, the cowboys catch sight of a herd of about 100 animals. Earl and his companions stop to check out the terrain. Three rocky outcrops rise in the north of the prairie. On the left is a dry riverbed, which they will follow so as to approach the

cattle from behind. Turning their horses to the right, the riders make a large circle and pretend to be going away again. Only momentarily disturbed by the riders' arrival, the cattle go back to their peaceful grazing.

Each of the men knows the position he must take up, and each knows that everything must be done calmly, with no shouting. Accidents can happen very suddenly. To prevent mishaps, certain rules must be observed. If the riders hem the cattle in too tightly, they may feel trapped and start to panic. The herd would then begin to circle, moving faster and faster and trampling the calves. If this turns into a stampede, there is only one thing that the cowboys can do, and that is ride straight into the furious maelstrom to break up the mass of horned beasts. As soon as a new group forms, the rest of the herd will join it and walk on quietly as before. Earl, though, is confident. This herd has never panicked and in four hours' time they should be back at the ranch.

THROUGHOUT THE WINTER, THE CATTLE ARE KEPT NEAR THE RANCH AND HAVE TO RECEIVE ADDITIONAL FOOD EVERY DAY. AS WINTER SETS IN, MUD BECOMES A PROBLEM FOR TRUCKS AND HAY IS TAKEN TO THE CATTLE BY HORSE AND CART.

FOLLOWING PAGES: TAKING PART IN THE FINAL HEAT OF THE LASSO-THROWING CONTEST IS ALWAYS AN ACHIEVEMENT. TRAVIS PUTS IN SOME PRACTICE SO THAT HE CAN JOIN ONE OF THE 24 TEAMS OF THREE RIDERS THAT WILL COMPETE IN A CORRAL. IN THE CALF-ROPING CONTEST, THE AIM IS TO LASSO A CALF IN RECORD TIME.

As the cows and their calves reach the ranch, lassos fly everywhere. One by one, the new calves are caught and branded. Travis wants to help but, with the cart ready hitched and the hay cut, there is other work for him to do in the fields. Ever since barbed wire was introduced in the 1870s, the cattle have spent the winter penned into pastures near the ranch. As the road network has grown, these pastures have become smaller than they once were, and many do not provide enough grazing. For several months in winter, the ground is also covered in a blanket of snow and the animals must be fed.

The cowboys of Montana spend most of their time on horseback, riding over the rough terrain of one of the last wild regions of the American West. The horses' hooves must be checked constantly. The ranches make all their own horseshoes, and there is no need for a visiting farrier as the cowboys themselves shoe their horses, shaping each shoe to the correct size for the horse.

ONCE THE CATTLE ARE PENNED INSIDE THE
CORRAL, THE COWBOYS START TO SEPARATE
THE CALVES FROM THE COWS.

By a wood fire in the evening, as the sounds of a guitar meld with gentle laughter, Travis listens to his neighbour's advice. He tells him that, before a horse can learn how to work cattle, it must get used to the whirring of the lasso above its head. After that, it can be taught how to behave once a cow has been lassoed, and how to brace against its furious thrashing, which varies according to whether it has been caught by the horns, the neck or the feet.

When Travis wakes up next morning, it is already seven o'clock and he should be out riding with the others. But no-one came to wake him; the ranch is silent and other sounds are muffled. As he rushes to the window he sees that everything is white, every blade of grass covered in thick snow. Travis knows the men must be in the barn putting studs on the horses' hooves. The dogs, a group of about 15 Border collies, run about and play in the snow. Like the Quarter Horses, these herding dogs, which the cowboys treat as friends, are excellent cattle drivers. The puppies learn directly from their mothers.

The dogs are taken to a pasture with livestock and, as the bitches work to their masters' commands, they also keep a close eye on the young dogs, nipping them if they start to play. Travis has often heard it said that a good dog can do the work of five cowboys.

By eight o'clock, with the snowfall easing, the cowboys and their dogs have set out. Hoof prints in the newly-fallen snow quickly lead them to the herds of cattle. The dogs are as agile and intelligent as the Quarter Horses, but they are also much lighter so they are less bothered by the snow, and are able to make extra efforts to help with the herding. This cooperation between animals is of great value to the cowboys. Travis loves those silent rides through the snowy landscape. There are no engines to be heard disturbing the peace. Nothing, not even the worst weather, stops the horses from going out. Smiling gently, the young man leans forward, hugs his horse's neck and whispers his gratitude. This 21st-century cowboy knows that his horse will carry him wherever he must go.

'EVERY COWBOY HAS HIS OWN HORSE HERE. NO-ONE EVER RIDES ANOTHER'S HORSE, UNLESS THERE IS REALLY NO OTHER OPTION. COWBOY AND HORSE WORK AS A TEAM — THAT'S VERY IMPORTANT FOR US. WITHOUT THE HORSES AND OUR DOGS, WE COULDN'T HERD THE CATTLE.' GLENNA STUCKY

ALL DAY TRAVIS CANTERS BACK AND FORTH, TWISTING AND TURNING AROUND THE CATTLE. EARL'S JOB IS TO LOOK OVER THE HERD TO MAKE SURE THAT EVERY ANIMAL BELONGS TO HIM. IF HE SEES ANY THAT ARE NOT HIS, TRAVIS WILL CATCH THEM WITH HIS LASSO.

After the great round-up, the calves are separated from their mothers and driven into corrals to be branded with the mark of the Stucky ranch. This allows the cattle to be identified in future and Earl will be able to find his herd the following autumn.

Following pages:
Horses never miss a thing, especially the sound of the cowboys' boots in the barn where the tack and the feed are kept!

THE BORDER COLLIE

In Montana, cowboys and their horses could not work without Border collies. These dogs were bred in Britain for herding sheep, and were brought to the Americas by settlers. Breeders and enthusiasts of Border collies ensure that the characteristics of the breed are maintained. Selection is rigorous, and the dogs and bitches that are mated are now chosen for their aptitude for working with cattle. With its keen sense of smell, the Border collie can follow herds even when their scent is under snow. Devoted to their master, alert, intelligent and easy to train, Border collies know instinctively how to work with the Quarter Horse. They are strong, keen, tenacious, hard-working and affectionate. Cowboys working in the prairies of Montana love their Border collies. They take a pack of dogs with them when they go out to round up a herd. The dogs can keep cattle in order merely by fixing them with their gaze, and so can control herds without close contact. A piercing look from a dog is enough to turn back a straying animal.

'BEING RAISED HERE, IN A FAMILY LIKE MINE,
YOU LEARN FROM EVERYONE. YOU ALSO LEARN
FROM YOUR MISTAKES, ESPECIALLY WHEN YOU
FALL OFF YOUR HORSE. IN THE END, LEARNING
FROM YOUR MISTAKES MAKE YOU BOUNCE BACK
QUICKER AND BECOME MORE RESILIENT.' TRAVIS

The Zaïane of the Middle Atlas

HERE, IN THE MIDDLE ATLAS MOUNTAINS OF MOROCCO, THE HARSH TERRAIN AND TRADITIONAL WAY OF LIFE APPEAR INTENSE, EVEN VIOLENT, TO THE OUTSIDER. IT IS AS THOUGH THE PEOPLE EXIST IN ANOTHER AGE, AND IT IS ESPECIALLY, A PLACE WHERE EVERYTHING BEGINS AND ENDS ON HORSEBACK. THE RIDER SEEN HERE IS A BERBER OF THE ZAÏANE TRIBE. HIS UPRIGHT SILHOUETTE COMPLEMENTS THE HORSE'S ELEGANTLY SLENDER, YET MUSCULAR NECK, ITS DAINTY SHOULDERS AND NARROW CHEST. ITS APPARENT FRAILTY HIDES AN EXTRAORDINARY STRENGTH. THE HORSES BORN IN THIS LAND OF RED EARTH, JAGGED MOUNTAINS AND EXTREMES OF TEMPERATURE MUST BE TOUGH TO SURVIVE.

The rider is called Mustapha, he is tall, with a light complexion and well-defined features. Mustapha makes an imposing figure in the saddle, he is the proud descendant of a desert people known as the Almoravids, who established a successful Berber dynasty in North Africa in the mid-11th century. The Berbers are believed to have inhabited the area since prehistoric times, they converted to Islam in 702 after fierce resistance to Arab expansion. The horsemen of the Middle Atlas are known as *Malous*, meaning 'sons of the shadow', their name sets them apart from the Berbers who live in the High Atlas, closer to the sun.

Mustapha's horse is an Arabian Barb. It carries its delicate head high and has a lithe build and elegant, graceful, almost floating paces. The breed origins of the Arabian Barb are disputed, it obviously carries Arab blood but the rest of its ancestry is

obscure, it may be a descendant of wild horses that lived in North Africa over 10,000 years ago.

The Berbers developed the breed, which is native to the Middle Atlas. The climate of the region features extremes of temperature and the terrain can be lush as well as stony – such conditions have produced a breed that is agile and sure-footed, with prodigious powers of endurance.

As he reaches the top of the hill, Mustapha leans back in the saddle and rests a hand on the damp neck of his horse, Adrar n'dern – the name means 'mountain of the mountains'. Horse and rider look down into the valley where the cultivated fields tuck themselves into the folds of the arid hills and then, with a gentle squeeze of his thighs, Mustapha urges the horse off down a steep path towards home. His cousin's wedding will be held this afternoon and he must get back to his family. In this region, it is the custom that a wedding is accompanied by a fantasia performed by local horsemen.

The horse's muscles ripple as he trots down the mountain daintily skimming over stones and avoiding the hazardous burrows hidden behind dry bushes. The sound of his hooves echoes off the rocks and rings out through the bright Moroccan air. His rider's hands on the reins hold him in check, otherwise he would break into an effortless canter that would bring them swiftly home.

OPPOSITE PAGE:
AN ANTIQUE STIRRUP IRON AND A HANDMADE SLIPPER ARE HERE COMBINED WITH DENIM JEANS AND A TRACKSUIT — MODERNITY VIES WITH TRADITION THE WORLD OVER.

ABOVE LEFT:
HORSEMEN THROUGHOUT THE WORLD KNOW THAT YOU MUST HOLD THE REINS AS GENTLY AS IF YOU WERE HOLDING A BABY BIRD IN EACH HAND.

ABOVE RIGHT:
'MY HORSE CAN GO WITHOUT FOOD OR WATER FOR A LONG TIME — UP TO TWO DAYS WITHOUT EATING OR DRINKING. HE ENJOYS BEING HOSED DOWN BUT HE DOESN'T LIKE GETTING HIS HEAD WET.' SAÏD

Mustapha has learnt from Saïd, the three fundamental items of value to the Zaïane
people, which form the basis of their culture: the horse, symbol of strength and
independence; the gun, which is fired in the name of freedom; and women, without
whom the tribe would become extinct. Mustapha and his father will now put on
their voluminous white jellabas, the costume of fantasia riders. The white cotton and
silk robes fly out behind the riders and they look as if their horses are carried on great
white wings.

The plain becomes filled with noise and bustle, and the sound of women singing. In their beguiling and inviting voices, accompanied by tambourines, they are singing songs of love and war known as the *Ahidou*.

Around the tents, the horses are tended by grooms who lovingly brush their silky coats to a sheen, so that, under the bright sunlight, they shine as brightly as earthly suns. When the bride is ready, they will be equipped with highly decorated saddles and bridles. The most important item is the richly coloured and brocaded velvet saddlecloth, which reaches the full length of the horse's back.

Arabian Barbs respond readily to the *Haffed Allah*, the *moqqadem*'s call. When they hear his cry, the horses take three restrained strides at a walk, then they surge forward, galloping headlong in a coordinated and orderly charge. As they fly along, their excited riders stand up in the stirrups. The horses put their hearts into the

The Bedouin of Wadi Rum

THE WADI RUM DESERT IN JORDAN IS A WILD PLACE. A RIDER APPEARS ON THE HORIZON, HE URGES HIS CAMEL TO AN UNWILLING CANTER BUT HE DOES NOT HAVE TIME TO REACH THE SHELTER OF THE ROCKS BEFORE A STRONG WIND SUDDENLY WHIPS UP THE SAND. THE BURNING, SANDY WIND HOWLS AS IT SWEEPS ACROSS THE EMPTY DESERT AND HE, AND HIS CAMEL, FALL HEAVILY. HE DOES NOT KNOW WHY THEY FELL, HE IS UNCONSCIOUS FOR SOME TIME BEFORE HE COMES ROUND AND REALISES THAT HIS CAMEL IS NOWHERE TO BE SEEN. LYING IN THE SAND, THE RIDER, IBRAHIM, FEELS A NAGGING PAIN IN HIS SHOULDER BUT HE DARE NOT MOVE. HIS LIPS ARE CRACKED AND HE IS THIRSTY, ALONE AND AFRAID. PAINFULLY HE RAISES HIS HEAD AND, IN A FOG OF OCHRE SAND, LOOKS AROUND. IN FRONT OF HIM IS EMPTINESS.

PREVIOUS PAGES:
BEDOUIN TRIBESMEN WITH CAMELS,
SHEEP AND HORSES TRAVELLING
ACROSS THE WADI RUM DESERT,
IN THE FAR SOUTH OF JORDAN.

ABOVE:
LIKE NOMADS ALL OVER THE WORLD,
THESE PEOPLE ARE SETTING UP CAMP.
THE TENTS ARE UNFOLDED AND SECURELY
PEGGED AGAINST SANDSTORMS.

OPPOSITE PAGE:
A HANDSOME, BEDOUIN BOY SMILES
SERENELY INTO THE CAMERA. HIS DEEP
BLACK, SHINING EYES SUGGEST A
CONTENTMENT WITH THE TRADITIONAL
WAY OF LIFE IN THE DESERTS OF
THE MIDDLE EAST.

Ibrahim was born here, into the Haueitate tribe and, like all Bedouin, he knows that the desert is a dangerous place for humans. He also knows that Trajan, his Arab stallion, would never have abandoned him. To stay with the rider, whatever happens, is one of the first things that the Bedouin teach their horses. Early on Ibrahim was taught this important survival technique by his uncle and his father. They practise by having a rider deliberately fall from his horse at a slow canter. A rope is attached to the horse's bridle and the rider keeps hold of this so that his weight slows and stops the horse. The Bedouin then reels the rope in, pulling the horse towards him and rewarding it by producing a lump of sugar from the pocket of his *gandura*. The exercise is repeated until the horse can be relied upon not to abandon its rider, a vital survival technique in the desert.

The origins of the Arab horse are unknown but horses of this type are recorded in artefacts from 2,500 years before the Christian era: in terms of genetics, the Arab is probably the purest breed in the world. Believed to have originated in Arabia, the Arab is a strong breed of horse suited to life in an arid climate. It is thin-skinned and has delicate, widely flaring nostrils that dilate to expel warm air, so keeping its body cool. The Bedouin cut the nasal cartilage to make it even easier for the horse to breathe. The Arab horse is renowned for its speed and endurance, according to Arabic legend, it was

created from a handful of wind that God mixed with his own breath. Another legend says that the Arab horse is descended from the five mares of Mohammed. The face of an Arab horse is unforgettable and very beautiful, its large, expressive eyes sit either side of the *jibbah*, a shield-shaped bulge of bone in the forehead which is unique to the breed. Its high tail carriage is also a unique characteristic of the Arab and is related to the fact that the breed has one fewer rib and two fewer tail vertebrae than other horses. Trajan, the horse that Ibrahim owns was bought for him by his father in the ancient city of Petra. There are hundreds of horses in the city, most of them are kept for tourists to ride but Trajan is too fine a horse for such a dreary life.

The Bedouin have a tradition of breeding camels as well as fine horses. Camels are capable of carrying loads over great distances, they can go without water for long periods, can live on the sparse desert vegetation and do not need intensive attention.

TOURISTS RIDE IN THE ANCIENT ROMAN CITY OF PETRA, UNDER THE SHADOWS OF THE GRAND FUNERARY TEMPLES CARVED INTO THE TOWERING ROCK FACE. TODAY, TOURISM IS AN IMPORTANT SOURCE OF REVENUE FOR THE BEDOUIN WHO ARE ABANDONING THEIR NOMADIC LIFESTYLE FOR LIFE IN THE TOWNS.

FOLLOWING PAGES:
'WE WON'T LOSE OUR CAMELS AS LONG AS WE HAVE HORSES. IF A CAMEL TRIES TO GET AWAY, WE SEND A RIDER TO BRING IT BACK TO THE CAMP.' IBRAHIM

They also provide a source of milk and meat. Horses, by contrast, need constant care, they must be fed and watered regularly, and so they have always been considered valuable, yet costly, animals to keep.

Ibrahim has managed to sit up. The storm seems to be passing and the wind has stopped howling, even though it is still whistling between fissures in the rock face. Debilitated by thirst, he can no longer trust his senses but above the howling of the wind he thinks he can hear the whinny of horses. Shadows pass before his eyes; perhaps he can make out the outline of two riders coming.

It is only when damp nostrils brush his face and seek out the pocket of his *gandura* that Ibrahim realises that he has been saved, because Trajan has guided his father to him. Hearing Kalil's strong voice thanking the horse for having rescued his son, the young man sinks into trusting slumber.

MINT TEA IS A TRADITIONAL PART OF BEDOUIN
CUISINE. THE NOMADIC BEDOUIN ARE MOST
AT HOME IN THE STILLNESS OF THE DESERT.

FOLLOWING PAGES:
'DRINKERS OF WIND' — AT A HEADLONG
GALLOP, WITH TAILS HELD HIGH, THESE
HORSES LIVE UP TO THIS DESCRIPTION.

'AS THE DESERT IS EMPTY OF EVERYTHING EXCEPT
SAND, GREAT IS THE PEACE TO BE FOUND THERE.'
HENRI MICHAUX, *Tranches de Savoir*

The Naadam Riders

SHE TRIES TO SWALLOW BUT SHE CANNOT. SHE IS OVERWHELMED BY A STRANGE PAIN IN HER THROAT AND FEELS HER EYES SMARTING. AS TEARS WELL UP, SHE RUBS HER EYES FURIOUSLY, SHE IS DETERMINED NOT TO CRY. ONORJARGAL HAS JUST TAKEN PART IN HER LAST *naadam*, THE LAST HORSE RACE SHE WILL EVER RIDE IN. SHE IS TOO OLD NOW, ALTHOUGH SHE IS STILL ONLY 13. THIS WAS HER LAST CHANCE TO WIN.

Onorjargal is in the family yurt, known in Mongolia as a *guer*, and although she knows every inch of the felt covering the wooden stakes she feels totally lost.

She gets to her feet, determined to overcome her exhaustion. She must somehow come to her senses, she must go out and face the vast Gal Shar plain. This Mongolian plain has been in her dreams since she was four years old but now it is the scene of her defeat.

Tied up to a rope between two stakes, ten of her grandfather's 60 horses, which are kept exclusively for racing, wait patiently. Since they were rounded up, they have undergone almost daily training. As part of the training routine, this young girl has put blankets over the horses to make them sweat and produce lean muscles. She has also run a sweat scraper over their coats and tasted their sweat to learn how to gauge the state of their health.

One of these horses is Koubilai, it is the horse she has just ridden in her very last race. As he stands there with his weight on three legs, resting a slightly trembling hind hoof, it is as if he is hardly breathing. With 600 other horses, he has just covered 25 miles (40 km), a 12.5 mile (20 km) ride to the starting point followed by a 12.5 mile (20 km) race back to the finishing line.

The horse feels that he is being watched and his eyes open slightly. The girl momentarily hesitates, torn between her desire to go to him or to stay in the *guer*.

ABOVE LEFT:

THE FRAME OF A *guer*, A TRADITIONAL TENT, BEFORE IT IS COVERED WITH SKINS. A *guer* CAN BE PUT UP AND TAKEN DOWN VERY QUICKLY.

ABOVE RIGHT:

THE ENTRANCE TO A *guer*. THE BAR FORMING THE THRESHOLD SHOULD NEVER BE TOUCHED. THIS CUSTOM IS A WAY OF MAKING PEOPLE WATCH THEIR STEP. SYMBOLICALLY IT IS A REMINDER THAT EVERY ACTION MUST BE A CONSCIOUS ONE.

OPPOSITE PAGE:

'MARE'S MILK IS A PART OF OUR STAPLE
DIET. WE DRINK IT, AND MAKE CHEESE
AND CREAM WITH IT.' ONORJARGAL

ABOVE:

WHILE THE MEN ARE OUT HERDING THE
HORSES WITH AN *urga*, A LONG LASSO,
THE WOMEN HAVE BEEN MAKING *airak*,
FERMENTED MARE'S MILK. TO STIMULATE
FERMENTATION, THE MILK IS POURED INTO
GOATSKINS. *Airak* IS BELIEVED TO HAVE
MEDICINAL PROPERTIES.

Onorjargal looks out at the immense plain where 20,000 horses are gathered. In orderly groups they surround the tents, which look like hundreds of white mushrooms. There are many other families of nomads here; they have come, like hers, to take part in the *naadam*. Accompanied by their yaks, horses and camels, some families have travelled more than 300 miles (500 km) to be here. Walking for several days and stopping where there is water, these families make such journeys with unfailing regularity. The great Gal Shar *naadam* takes place once every four years and the winner of each race holds the title and therefore the renown of the family's herd until the next *naadam*. Onorjargal's thoughts are interrupted by a familiar voice. Dodja, her younger sister, who is five, is about to enter the family *guer*. She skips along humming a little Buddhist song of the sort that every Mongol child knows and, as she goes in, she brushes against a wooden barrel filled with *airak* – fermented mare's milk, which is a staple in the Mongolian diet and of which Mongols are extremely fond.

Onorjargal feels pangs of hunger but her disappointment stops her eating. She goes over to Koubilai to see if he needs anything. Like others of his breed, this three-year-old horse is small with a compact frame.

His thick tail touches the ground. The young girl stands close to him but she does not speak. The great empty expanses and the penetrating cold are not conducive to

chattiness. She looks at the horse, closes her eyes and relives this morning's events. She remembers her mother helping her to get ready and lovingly tying on her number, which was 808. Then she was surrounded by 600 other competitors. Most were aged between seven and eleven, and those that were older, like Onorjargal, were light for their age. While some chose to ride bareback so as to lessen the weight that their horses must carry, most preferred the comfort of a saddle.

Onorjargal's race was for three-year-old horses. Onorjargal remembers adjusting the number tied to her back and trying to move away from the seething mass of horses, but she was immediately driven back by a man in red who was waving a whip. The man was one of several stewards who were trying to keep the herd of screaming horses together, aware that many of the young jockeys would use tricks to help them win. A favourite trick is to wait for the chance to wheel around and then gallop off towards the finishing line as though they could not hold their horse back, a ruse that will not disqualify them. Amid the men's curses and flying whips, the race begins under great pressure. Onorjargal knew that she had to hold Koubilai back so as to preserve his energy. Like all the other children, she sang the *Ginko* as she rode, this is the first song that young riders learn. In Mongolia, singing is as natural as breathing.

OPPOSITE PAGE AND ABOVE RIGHT:
EVERY GENERATION TAKES A STEP CLOSER
TO THE MODERN WORLD. THE YOUNG
MONGOL MAN ON THE LEFT IS CASUAL AND
RELAXED ASTRIDE A GLEAMING MOTORBIKE
BUT THE OLD MAN, DRESSED IN A RED *del*,
IN THE PICTURE ABOVE, EXAMINES IT ONLY
FROM A DISTANCE.

ABOVE LEFT:
ONORJARGAL PREPARES TO EXERCISE A
HORSE. 'IT'S ESSENTIAL TO LEARN TO
RIDE WHEN YOU'RE VERY YOUNG, AS
YOU'RE QUITE LIGHT THEN AND DON'T
TIRE THE HORSE OUT.' ONORJARGAL

THE PROCESS OF TURNING WILD HORSES
INTO RIDING HORSES IS DONE WITH BARE
HANDS AND BY BRUTE FORCE.

'AFTER A HORSE HAS RACED, WE RUN A WOODEN SWEAT SCRAPER ALL OVER ITS COAT. WE THEN EXAMINE THE HORSE'S SWEAT, AND SOMETIMES WE TASTE IT, TO SEE WHETHER THE HORSE IS IN GOOD HEALTH. MANY SWEAT SCRAPERS ARE DECORATIVELY CARVED.' OUKHNAA

ONE OF THE MEN SHOWN HERE WEARS A CLOTH WITH A NUMBER ON IT ROUND HIS WAIST. THIS WAS THE NUMBER HE WORE WHEN HE WON A RACE AS A CHILD.

Onorjargal remembers how the starting line – marked by nothing more than a rope held taught by two men – suddenly came into view a short distance ahead. The first 400 horses were already there, jostling each other so as to be among the first away.

Seeing what was about to happen, Onorjargal sat up and, tightly gripping the reins in one hand, was on the point of turning Koubilai around. But it was too late, the horses were already off and as they galloped towards her, she was caught by the onslaught. The Mongolian horse can cover 75 miles (120 km) in a day with a rider on its back. Races such as the Gal Shar *naadam* bring out the horse's best qualities, prove its endurance and stamina and its ability to stand up to the test. Galloping over rough ground is risky, so the rider must concentrate on steering the horse rather than urging

it on. Onorjargal was knocked over by a riderless horse, his young rider having fallen earlier. It is important for riders to look out for loose horses, their herding instinct keeps them in the race even though they are riderless and they may bump into another horse and cause it to fall. The winning horse must always cross the finishing line carrying a rider but riderless horses who come in after the winner are placed according to how they finish.

Onorjargal is startled from her thoughts as she feel a hand on her shoulder. Oukhnaa, her grandfather, is right beside her. He holds an *urga*, a kind of flexible stick made up of several pieces of wood bound together with leather. The Mongols use *urgas* to catch young horses. Oukhnaa, has come up beside her without a sound. On his feet are skin boots with pointed, upward-curling toes and he wears a *del*, a long silk tunic that is the

THE NUMBERS FOR EACH RACE ARE INDIVIDUALLY HAND-PAINTED. THERE ARE AS MANY AS 20 RACES EACH YEAR AND EACH MAY HAVE HUNDREDS OF COMPETITORS.

ONORJARGAL'S GRANDFATHER BURNS INCENSE WHICH HE BELIEVES WILL MAKE THE HORSES BRAVE. SHE FOLLOWS BEHIND, THROWING SPOONFULS OF FERMENTED MILK AT THEIR FEET, TO BRING THEM GOOD LUCK DURING THE RACE.

traditional dress of Mongol warriors. His weather-beaten face, marked by sun, wind and frost, betrays no emotion – neither disappointment nor a questioning look.

As a wave of love and gratitude sweeps over her, Onorjargal does not lower her eyes. This man is not only her grandfather but a noble descendant of the warriors of Temujin, otherwise known as Genghis Khan. He is an *arat*, a shepherd, the embodiment of a people who are proud to be outnumbered by horses on their territory. At the appropriate season each year he leads his family to and from the *ail*, the term for the grass that covers the vast steppes and that is food for the horses which are his pride and his glory.

For a thousand years, Mongol tradition has dictated that men enter the world in a *guer* and die on horseback. The legendary vigour of the horsemen who fought in the armies of Temujin has been passed down through the generations. Without their horses, with

their extraordinary hardiness and endurance, these armies, drawn from the people of the steppes, could not have forced the civilised, sedentary peoples of the Middle East and Europe into submission. These well-organized and terrifying conquerors established the world's largest-ever land-based empire, which stretched from the shores of the Pacific to the Danube, and from the Persian Gulf to the Arctic Circle.

Not a word has been spoken but Onorjargal knows what she must do. As if by magic her exhaustion has lifted, she takes a horse, unties the nine others and sets off alone to the spring. She looks back at her grandfather, the man who has taught her everything about horses. He is sprinkling fermented milk in her wake, a symbolic and spiritual act to ensure that good luck will follow her. Onorjargal understands, she stops the horses and, with a firm voice, calls Dodja, her little sister. It is time that she was taught to ride.

THE COLOUR BLUE HAS A SACRED SIGNIFICANCE TO MONGOLS AND SO OUKHNAA ADDS A THIN BLUE RIBBON TO HIS HORSE'S HEADPIECE. BLUE SIGNIFIES A PRAYER FOR VICTORY. WHEN THE PREPARATORY RITUALS HAVE BEEN PERFORMED, THE YOUNG RIDERS AND THEIR HORSES MAKE THEIR WAY TO THE STARTING LINE.

THE NAADAM

WOMEN DRESS THE YOUNG
JOCKEYS BEFORE THEY GO
DOWN TO THE FINISHING LINE.
THE RACE BEGINS WITH A SLOW TROT
TO THE OFFICIAL STARTING POINT,
WHICH CAN BE 12.5 MILES (20 KM)
AWAY. THE RACE IS RUN OVER THE
SAME GROUND BACK TO THE
FINISHING LINE.

'Naadam' is the Mongol word for 'fair'. Wherever these festivities
take place, families from all over Mongolia flock to them with great
excitement and enthusiasm. They are occasions when the history of
their people is celebrated and the renown of their herds demonstrated.
Although the Gal Shar *naadam* takes place only once every four years,
other fairs are held at more frequent intervals. The Ulan Bator *naadam*,
for example, is held every year, on 11 July. A naadam involves many
types of competition. As well as the celebrated horse races, there are
wrestling matches and archery contests. The wrestling matches are
among the oldest games of the steppe; they were held by the warriors
of Temujin, the Mongol emperor in the early 13th century when his
invincible cavalry swept across

central Asia. Wrestling matches are a focus for gambling, bets are taken on the outcome of contests in which the aim is to bring the opponent to the ground. The victor is presented with a medal bestowing on him the title of People's Hero. Horse races are still central to the events, although gleaming motorbikes are beginning to replace some of the horses on the steppes. Thousands of Mongols gather in huge crowds at the finishing line of the races to find out who is the winner. To win one of these highly prestigious races is a great honour and the winners' herds will be celebrated for the whole of the following year, or for as many as four years, in the case of the Gal Shar *naadam*. The archery contests have an almost feverish following. The mounted archer takes up his bow and quiver as

WITH ALL THEIR STRENGTH, THE MEN HOLDING THE STARTING LINE TUG ON THE ROPE TO HOLD BACK THE 600 COMPETITORS BUT THEIR EFFORTS ARE IN VAIN. THE ROPE SNAPS AND THE RIDERS SURGE FORWARDS.

PAGES 210–211
LEFT: ONLY ONE OF THESE THREE HORSES STILL HAS ITS RIDER, BUT THE TWO RIDERLESS HORSES WILL NOT BE DISQUALIFIED. RIGHT: THE HORSE THAT THIS NINE-YEAR-OLD GIRL IS RIDING WEARS THE BLUE SASH THAT IS BESTOWED ON THE WINNER.

if they were sacred objects and, concentrating hard, aims three arrows
at the ivory circles in the centre of a target, 250 feet (70 metres) in
front of him. To the Mongols, archery is a sport with a spiritual
dimension involving the twin symbols of the Mongol people,
the bow and the horse. These symbols recall the terror that their
ancestors inspired 700 years ago across the entire continent of Asia.

'WE COULDN'T SURVIVE WITHOUT HORSES. WE HERD
WITH THEM, WE USE THEM TO CARRY OUR FAMILIES,
THEY PROVIDE US WITH MILK AND WE BURN THEIR
DROPPINGS, WHICH GIVES US HEAT AND FLAME FOR
COOKING OUR FOOD. THE WIND ON THE STEPPE
PREVENTS TREES FROM GROWING SO WE CANNOT USE
WOOD. LIFE WOULD BE QUITE IMPOSSIBLE WITHOUT
HORSES.' OUKHNAA

The Gauchos of Patagonia

AS HE CAME TOWARDS ME, THIS LITTLE BOY WITH A SMILING FACE AND
PENETRATING, SPELLBINDING YET FRIENDLY EYES. HE WAS SO CALM AND
SO EPHEMERAL THAT HE WAS ALMOST UNREAL. EVEN THE SHADE OF HIS HAT
COULD NOT DIM THE CHEERFUL BRIGHTNESS OF HIS DEEP BROWN EYES.
YET, I WILL NEVER FORGET THE OVERWHELMING, UNEASY FEELING THAT
I HAD HAD BEFORE THIS MEETING, WHICH FILLED EVERY STEP ALONG THE WAY
THROUGH LAND THAT SEEMED TO STRETCH TO INFINITY. PATAGONIA IS A COUNTRY
WHERE ANOTHER, VERY DIFFERENT WORLD BEGINS; THOSE WHO EXPERIENCE IT
ARE CHANGED BY IT. I FOUND ANSWERS TO PREVIOUSLY UNFATHOMABLE
QUESTIONS IN MY TIME AMONG THESE HORSE RIDING PEOPLE.

'WE EDUCATE OUR CHILDREN VERY
LOVINGLY HERE. NO-ONE WOULD WANT
THEM TO BE IN A TOWN. I KNOW WHAT
TOWNS ARE LIKE AND THAT'S WHY
I KNOW THAT THEIR FUTURE IS HERE,
CLOSE TO NATURE.' JULIO

Patagonia stole my heart, I found it a bewitching land and it has enslaved me for ever.

As I stand stock still beside my car, on the only road between Neuquen and Anda Collo, I acknowledge the slight hand sign that the child makes. It took time to get used to the fact that gauchos always greet you when they come across you.

Following this small child, who was to play such an important role in my future, comes a horse, brown like the foothills of the Andean cordillera. Easy and relaxed, the reins hooked over the pommel, it follows the boy as he walks along. Chewing on its bit, the horse never takes its eyes off the little boy walking in front, both hands thrust deep in the pockets of his old anorak. The horse is free to gallop away at any moment, but its docile behaviour leads me to wonder where stories of the legendary brutality of the Gauchos of Patagonia have come from.

As he walks up to me, he holds out a hand; his handshake is surprisingly firm for a boy of ten. He was waiting for me. His father, who is busy back at the livestock farm, sent him to meet me. Miko introduces me to his horse, El Gringo, in just the same way that he would later introduce me to his brother. He mounts El Gringo and invites me to follow him.

Along the way I reflect on all those people who live 'for', 'with' or 'thanks to' horses. They have all warmly welcomed me into their lives, entrusting their deepest selves and often that of their horses to the camera lens, frequently forgetting my presence among them, and my purpose in recording their lives, and smiling at my arrogant, and sometimes inept, curiosity.

Julio, Miko's father, is a gaucho, no different from any other, except that our paths happen to have crossed. Like all gauchos, he has a striking personal stature and great respect for other people. Father and son have given me their trust quite unpretentiously, and have

219

his hopes, his courage and his will to go on. Nature can deliver fierce blows, but because he lives close to nature, Julio understood that he must pick himself up and start afresh. Today he has 3,000 goats. His courage in the face of adversity was a lesson to me. While Miko told me all about his people's heritage, it was the horses that gave me the key to understanding him.

The past, however glorious or victorious, is almost irrelevant in this part of the world, where each new day must be taken as a new beginning. Discovering whether Argentine horses have Spanish or Arab blood is a matter of little importance. Their existence today seems unconnected to the 16th-century conquistador, Cortes who first brought horses to the New World. As I enjoyed seeing the herds wandering in complete freedom, seeking to find out about them from the pages of dusty books seemed to me laughable. The fact that they still live and flourish in this land today is due to their

ABOVE: MIKO AND HIS HORSE, EL GRINGO. 'I WOULDN'T LIKE TO LIVE IN A TOWN BECAUSE THERE'S NO ROOM FOR ANIMALS THERE, ESPECIALLY NOT FOR HORSES, SO I COULDN'T BE WITH THEM ANY MORE. THEY WOULDN'T BE FREE IN A TOWN AND I'D LOSE MY FREEDOM TOO. WITHOUT A HORSE I COULDN'T GO GALLOPING OFF WHENEVER I FELT LIKE IT, OR GO DOWN TO THE RIVER TO SOAK THE LASSOS.' MIKO

impressive ability to adapt to living in a new environment, where they were abandoned by the Spanish adventurers.

The story that Miko has to tell is poetic. I can still hear his voice quivering as he spoke about the wild horses that found a paradise in this permanently snowy land. His story glorifies and immortalises the life of the Mapuche Indians, the original inhabitants of Patagonia, who were attacked and killed by the Spaniards. In time, they have been revenged and their spirit now fills the vast plains of Patagonia. There is a quiver in Miko's voice as he recalls the puma that would kill 14 dogs to protect its lair, and it soars as he tells of the condors that are kept away from the herds by the smoke of fires. For him, the past is a living history because it is always connected to horses and to nature, and because it is kept alive by constant retelling. Wherever life takes him, Miko owes his life's journey to his horse.

El Gringo, Tordo and all the other horses are the custodians of these men's survival. Their breed is Criollo and their physique shows that they have adapted to the rigours of life on the cordillera. Slightly stockier than their relatives on the pampas, they have sturdy legs and tougher hooves, and are better balanced for the tasks required of them.

Tordo, is Julio's close companion and is almost like a brother to him. When they are not working together around the herds, Tordo is free, never being tethered or hobbled, and he always responds to Julio's whistling call with obvious happiness. He has not been trained to obey but to share. He is ignorant of pirouettes, extended trots, or passage, the sideways walk of dressage, but he moves with a natural grace that owes little to human tutelage. In this relationship, it is hard to tell who is the master, the gaucho or the horse. Horse and rider operate as a team that drives, steers and rules over the herd of 3,000 unruly, nimble and flighty goats.

'TRANSHUMANCE IS A TRADITION THAT GOES BACK MORE THAN 200 YEARS. WE SPEND LONG PERIODS OF TIME AWAY FROM OUR FAMILIES. THAT'S HARD, BUT WE MUST DO IT FOR THE HERDS. THE ANIMALS NEED THE GRAZING.' JULIO

Acknowledgements

I would like to thank Hazan, the publishers who have, metaphorically, ridden alongside me on this great trek; Élodie, who joined my venture with fearlessness and enthusiasm; Anne-Isabelle, whose firmness and gentleness would make her an excellent rider, and whose guidance and support through tribulation ultimately gave me remarkable freedom. I also thank François and my family, who selflessly bore with me for over a year, and all those who, like me, feel that they do not live 'in the world of the horse' rather, it is the spirit of the horse that live within us.

Sylvie Lebreton

Ampersand would like to thank the producers Philippe Allante, Rebecca Boulanger, Didier Fassio, Sylvie Lebreton and Laure Poinsot, as well as Anne Mariage (Cheval d'Aventure), Jean-Louis Gouraud, Yves Bruezière (Equidia) and Ann Julienne (La Cinquième).

Other books by Tibo

Le Hutteau, Portraits de Chasseurs en Baie de Somme
Éditions Martelle, 1999 – ISBN 2 89870 076 6

Portraits de Côtes, Entre Baie de Somme et Rye Bay
Éditions Martelle, 2001 – ISBN 2 87890 083 9

This book accompanied the documentary television series
Les Cavaliers du Mythe, produced by Ampersand

First published by Hazan, an imprint of Hachette-Livre
43 Quai de Grenelle, Paris 75905, Cedex 15, France
© 2001 Édition Hazan
Under the title *Les Cavaliers du Mythe*
All rights reserved

Project editors: Anne-Isabelle Vannier and Élodie Fondacci
Design: Tibo, F-80120 Villiers-sur-Authie
http://www.tibo.org
and Sylvie Creuze
35 mm photography using Kodak Portra negative film
and Hasselblad, Mamiya and Leica M6 equipment
Photographs printed by Sandra/Picto Bastille
Ampersand: Jean Dufour, Fabrice Estève, Philippe Geyer, Nathalie
Giboire-Labid and Gilles Thion.

Reproduction: Label Image, Saint-Omer
http://www.labelimage.net
Printed in Italy by Rotolito Lombarda

Language translation produced by Translate-A-Book, Oxford

© 2003 English translation, Octopus Publishing Group Ltd, London
This edition published by Hachette Illustrated UK,
Octopus Publishing Group, 2-4 Heron Quays, London, E14 4JP

Printed by Tien Wah, Singapore

ISBN: 1-84430-029-3